THE BIG BOOK OF

FAMILY GATHERINGS

for Parish Faith Formation

THE BIG BOOK OF FAMILY GATHERINGS

for Parish Faith Formation

Judy Elliott Dantzer

Illustrated by Kris Flechsig Myers

Our Sunday Visitor Publishing Division
Our Sunday Visitor, Inc.
Huntington, Indiana 46750

Nihil Obstat
Rev. Michael Heintz
Censor Librorum

Imprimatur
✠ John M. D'Arcy
Bishop of Fort Wayne-South Bend
December 13, 2006

Our Sunday Visitor Publishing Division
Our Sunday Visitor, Inc.
200 Noll Plaza
Huntington, IN 46750

ISBN 978-1-59276-266-8 (Inventory No. X321)

Cover design by Tyler Ottinger
Interior design by Sherri L. Hoffman

PRINTED IN THE UNITED STATES OF AMERICA

Contents

Contents

Introduction

What is a Family Gathering?

A Family Gathering is a simple format of gathering parents and children to focus in fun, creative ways on a religious theme or topic. It teaches through hands-on participation in prayer, skits, crafts, games, and activities. It involves *everyone* and provides lasting take-home projects to remind parents and children alike the message taught. It is intergenerational — seniors enjoy the sense of excitement and often lend a helping hand with the projects. Junior and Senior High youth are enthused about being involved in the skits or helping prepare or clean up the craft areas. Parents love the fact that their children are associating "Church" with words like "Wow!" And most importantly, there is a definite feeling of belonging, of a growing identity with the parish community. With parishes struggling with a distinction of "School Family" or "Religious Education" family, these Family Gatherings provide great opportunities to create a sense of unity and oneness.

How do we get started?

Open the book, select the theme and begin! Everything — activities, crafts, plays, scripts, supplies, and refreshment suggestions are provided to ensure your success! The first decision to make is *what time* would work best in your parish. Gatherings may be held any time of the day or week. They are designed to last around one to two hours, depending on the number of crafts or activities you choose to select, and how patient you are with little ones who just can't seem to get enough glitter on their project.

What do we need (space, money, leadership)?

You select the activities and crafts to suit the meeting space you have. It works well to use multiple rooms if they are available to add to the excitement, but one area works also. The cost of all suggested materials presented in this manual is minimal. They were designed and used in parish settings where the budget was very limited.

Leadership? This is a wonderful benefit! With the growing excitement of this form of ministry, leadership develops on multiple levels. Some individuals may volunteer to do the art work, some provide the publicity, and others help with the refreshments or collect the needed craft items. You may begin alone, but soon you will be brainstorming future events with a "team of many" — guaranteed!

Who developed these Family Gatherings?

Judy has worked in the Archdiocese of Detroit for 20 years as a youth minister and Director of Religious Education and is now a Pastoral Associate at Our Lady of La Salette Parish in

Introduction

Berkley, Michigan. Kris is a former commercial artist, a wonderfully gifted catechist of many years, and is also employed in the Religious Education Department at Our Lady of La Salette.

Have these Family Gatherings been successfully used?

We schedule our Family Gatherings on the third Sunday of each month, immediately following the Sunday morning Mass. They last around one to one and a half hours. We have completed four years of Gatherings, holding one each month from September through May. The benefit to our parish community has been tremendous — all ages welcome, involved, and excited to be together!

What options do we have?

As religious educators explore various avenues for evangelization and formation, these Family Gatherings may be a first step. They serve very effectively as an outreach to families who may have been away from the Church for a while. Parents in schools and neighborhoods invite one another to activities their children enjoy. Once the children are connected, the parents will follow. The ideas and projects of this manual may also be used in the individual classroom. In addition, with the growing movement toward whole community catechesis, they may be adapted to include a specific adult formation piece.

In every parish community, there are some families for whom a weekly commitment to religious education classes may be impossible due to a variety of reasons. These Family Gatherings may fill the void of catechesis not only in the children's lives, but also in the parents' lives.

The options are many! Let's get started!

1. ADVENT

Objective:
To reinforce a reverent image of the Nativity.

Setting:
Participants' tables face a simple scene: A life-size, hay-filled manger (crate, cardboard, or a doll crib camouflaged with brown paper) centered in front of a stable (trellis, cardboard box cave, or paper backdrop) flanked by potted plants. A wide aisle through the center of the tables is lined with white tube lights leading to an empty manger. The room lights are subdued and soft music is played in the background to promote a reverent tone as people are quietly ushered in.

Separate table is set for the "Baby Jesus in the Manger" craft, and it and the refreshment table remain covered until after the presentation.

Activity Summary:
Hosts greet and usher the families in. One or more readers (up to four) present the story, pausing for a child to bring an item up from their table and place it on "stage." Costumed "Mary" and "Joseph" also come forward at the appropriate time. At the end of the story, parents and children draw a picture of their family on a heart and place it in the manger. Then the families move to the craft and refreshment areas.

Supplies:
- A large Bible.
- White tube lights.
- Each table has a tablecloth, a sprig of greenery, and at least one of the following items: rings, rolled scroll, candle, lighthouse, angel wings, haloes, wrapped gift, rocks, donkey, light colored cloth for bedding, small amount of straw, baby doll, star, gold, frankincense, myrrh, shepherd's hook, sheep or lamb, crown, magnifying glass.
- Costumes for Mary and Joseph.
- Enough red hearts for each family or each child, and markers or crayons.

Advent

Script:

Reader #1: Hundreds of years before Jesus was born, the prophet Isaiah told people a Savior was coming. Isaiah was a prophet who shared God's message with his people.

Reader #2: (Lifts up a large Bible and then reads Isaiah 9:2, 6-7.)

Reader #1: What was Isaiah's message? God promised to send His Son, who would be the Light of the World.

(Reader #2 will light a large candle next to where the Bible is placed.)

Reader #1: In Isaiah, God calls Jesus a covenant. In the time when Jesus lived, people entered into a covenant when they made an agreement to help each other. They exchanged rings or a written pledge on paper to show they would never break their promise. God's promise to us is that His Son, Jesus would be born to be the Light of the World. God's promise is that Jesus came to show us how to love each other.

Reader #2: Please bring the rings and the promise scroll and place them near the manger.

Reader #3: Have you ever tried to walk in the dark? Did you trip, and maybe felt afraid? The Light of Jesus will always shine before us to lead us to safety. He is like a lighthouse. Lighthouses lead ships to safety and warn sailors of dangerous rocks ahead.

Reader #2: Please bring the candle light and the lighthouse to the manger.

Reader #4: God spoke through the angels to tell people the Good News. They spoke to Mary and to Joseph to tell them that Jesus was about to be born. God's angels are all around us to guide us, to protect us, and to comfort us.

Reader #2: When we are afraid, help us to remember our guardian angels. Please bring the angels to the manger. (Wings and haloes)

Reader #1: God had a very special purpose for a young girl named Mary. He spoke to her through the angel Gabriel. Mary trusted in God and obeyed Him with all her heart. She said, "Yes, Lord, let it be according to your will."

(Mary will come forward and sit or stand near the manger.)

Reader #3: When we know we will soon be opening a wonderful present, it is hard to wait. Imagine how Mary must have felt, knowing the baby Jesus was growing inside her. She longed to see what He would be like.

Reader #2: Please bring the wrapped gift to the manger.

Reader #4: An angel of the Lord appeared to Joseph and asked him to take Mary as his wife. God chose Joseph, a good and kind man, a carpenter, to be the foster Father of Jesus.

(Joseph will come forward and sit or stand near the manger.)

Reader #3: Around the time that Jesus was to be born, the ruler of the Jewish people ordered everyone to travel to the city of their families' ancestors to be counted. Joseph and Mary had to go to Bethlehem, a distance of 70 miles. It was a long and hard journey over rocky paths with Mary riding on a donkey.

Reader #2: Please bring the rocks and the donkey to the manger.

Reader #1: Each of us needs to prepare a place in our hearts for Jesus. He will come to us and we need to make our world ready to receive Him.

Reader #4: Please bring the cloth for the manger.

Reader #3: (*Holding the Bible high, then, reading the passage from it.*) "The time came for Mary to have her child, and she gave birth to her firstborn son. She wrapped him in swaddling clothes and laid Him in a manger, because there was no room for them in the inn."

(*Mary or Reader #1 takes the doll from a hidden spot and places the baby into the manger.*)

Reader #2: God set His star in the sky to lead the first gift-givers to the infant Jesus. God gave the gift of His Son, and the Wise Men gave the gift of their treasures. The Wise Men gave gifts of gold, frankincense, and myrrh. What extra meaning did these gifts have? Gold is the most precious of metals; only powerful kings had great storehouses of gold. Frankincense comes from tree sap and, when it is burned, gives off a wonderful, spicy smell, like incense used in worship. Myrrh is a fragrance also. It is used during burials. Through these gifts, the Wise Men declared that Jesus was King, God, and Savior.

Reader #1: Please bring forward the star that led the way to Jesus and the gifts of gold, frankincense, and myrrh.

Reader #4: Who is missing from our manger? (Pause) "Now there were shepherds living in the fields, keeping night watch over their sheep. An angel of the Lord appeared to them and said, 'Do not be afraid, for today a Savior has been born.'" What made God choose shepherds, out of all the people in Bethlehem? God knew that shepherds would not ask questions. They simply listened and believed and quickly went out to find Jesus. Are we like that? Are we in a hurry to find Jesus?

Reader #3: Please bring the shepherd's hook and the sheep forward and place them near the manger.

Reader #2: There are three items we have yet to bring to the manger. Please bring forward the crown. The crown tells us that Jesus is King of the world, King of our lives.

Please bring forward the magnifying glass. Jesus seeks what is lost. He looks at us with eyes that see us very clearly.

Pick up the red heart that is on each table. The heart represents love. Jesus is love. He loves us very much. Now, we ask everyone to draw a simple picture of themselves and place it in the manger. Let this be the present you give the baby Jesus this Christmas — the gift of your family's love.

"Baby Jesus in the Manger" Craft:

Supplies (For each craft)
- One 6" X 3" envelope (or larger) with the top flap removed
- 4 popsicle sticks
- 1 star
- 1 foam (or cardboard) rectangle cut 6" X 3"
- Yarn
- Crayons
- Glue and glue applicators
- Baby Jesus template

Directions

Color the envelope (manger) and the Baby
    Jesus.

Glue the foam or cardboard rectangle to the
    back of the envelope (manger).

Glue two popsicle sticks into the "manger" for
    roof supports.

Glue two more sticks on, touching at the top to
    form a roof.

Cut up yarn ("straw") and add with glue in the
    "manger."

Glue the star to the top of the roof.

Place Baby Jesus inside the "manger."

Refreshments:

Christmas cookies, coffee, cocoa

2. JOURNEY TO THE LIGHT OF JESUS

Objective:

To focus families on the real message of the season as we actively prepare ourselves to welcome Christ.

Setting:

Tables and chairs arranged with the tables covered to protect from glue spills. One table is prepared for glitter application, another available for the straw to be glued, and another for the making of the Advent Candle.

A center microphone for our readers (older teens would be excellent to play the roles in the script).

Activity Summary:

The families gather to hear the stories of Mary, Joseph, the Angels, Shepherds, and Kings. Then they are given a "baggie" of these figures and outlines of sheep, a cow, a manger, and a star. They are also given a large round pizza cardboard that has been covered with dark paper with the letters in the center or across the top — "Journey to the Light of Jesus." In addition, they receive a "baggie" with the items needed to decorate all these figures and complete this "Advent Wheel."

If desired, a simple candleholder with candle can also be created to place in the middle of this wheel.

Script Supplies:

Actors: Mary, Joseph, Shepherd, King, Angel
Costumes for the characters if possible (different head wraps might do!)

Script:

Narrator: We all can relate to the busyness of shopping and holiday preparations — yet today we want to focus on the real meaning of this season: the journey we all share of preparing ourselves to welcome the Light of Jesus into our lives and into our world. It is our hope that the craft the children will be making today brings this message home to them. First, we have some special visitors to tell you their story.

Mary: Hello, boys and girls, my name is Mary, the Mother of Jesus.

I lived in the town of Nazareth with my parents Ann and Joachim. When I was a teenager, I became engaged to a wonderful man named Joseph. We were to be married soon, but before we were married, a miracle happened!

I was in my room in my parent's home when all of a sudden an angel appeared before me. The angel said his name was Gabriel and that I should not be afraid of him. "Hail Mary, full of grace!" he said. I did not know what to think! Imagine that God would send an angel to me! The angel began to speak again, saying that he was sent by God to announce Our Savior's coming — and that I was to be the Messiah's Mother! How could I be the Mother of God's Son? I could not under-stand why God would choose me, but I said to the angel, "God's will be done." I knew that God had chosen me, and I would do anything that He asked me to. Think, boys and girls — that God asks you to do things also. He wants each of us to bring the Love of Jesus to others.

Remember my "yes" to God brought Jesus into the world — your "yes" to God will bring Jesus to others.

Joseph: I am Joseph, the foster Father of Jesus and the husband of Mary. I was a carpenter in our village of Nazareth. Our lives centered on our faith in God and on the hope that one day our Messiah would come to bring true peace and freedom to our people.

I was not a young man, yet I was still unmarried. I was introduced to Mary, a young girl of 15. I had never seen someone so beautiful and gentle! We were engaged to be married. I thought my life couldn't be any better! Before we were married, I found out Mary was going to have a baby. An angel of the Lord came to me in a dream, and said, "Joseph, do not be afraid to take Mary home as your wife. She will give birth to a son and you must name him Jesus — He is the One sent by God to save all people from their sins." I was so honored by God to care for His Son and my young wife, Mary.

Boys and girls, when Jesus was a young man in Nazareth, children would run after him saying, "Jesus, what story do you have for us today?" He loved to sit surround-ed by young children and tell them stories.

Ask Jesus to come into your life in a new way this Advent season. Gather at His feet like the children in Nazareth so long ago, and hear His stories and know how much He loves you.

Narrator: Let's listen to what others have to tell us about the birth of Jesus.

(You may or may not wish to use the following additional scripts, along with the Narrator's message.)

The Shepherd: We were in the hills that night guarding our sheep. The life of a shepherd is a very busy one — always looking for those young sheep that wander away and get caught in thorny brambles — or are lost without water to drink. It seems like we shepherds are always looking down at the ground — checking to see if there is enough grass for our sheep to eat. That is why on the night that Jesus was born, — we were amazed when the sky lit up with angels — beautiful angels — telling us "Do not be afraid! We bring you good news! The Savior of the world has been born tonight!" We had to leave immediately and find Him. Seeing the infant Jesus changed our lives forever! God gave Love to the world that night!

Narrator: The shepherds had nothing to give to the baby Jesus. They came empty handed to the stable — just to look at Jesus and to love Him. Many times, we too may feel we have nothing to give to Jesus, but like the shepherds, we can simply come to Jesus with our prayers, and love Him in our hearts. The shepherds were simple people — but they were open to the unexpected — they listened to the angels' message and they went to find Jesus.

Do we look for the angels telling us a message from God — or are we too busy to hear?

The Three Kings: We have traveled very, very far — through unfamiliar places with foreign people. It seemed like we would never come to the end of our journey — yes, we grew tired, but we were determined to find the newborn King of the Jews! When we saw that bright star rest over the small stable, we were so excited! In one way our journey was over — and in another way our journey of faith had just begun!

Narrator: Like the three kings, we too travel each day. Maybe it is only to school, or to work, yet we look for the face of Jesus in each person we meet, and we see the wonder of God in the world around us.

The Angels: On that beautiful night, we sang to the shepherds of the birth of our Savior, Jesus! We brought Good News to the world — do not be afraid, God has sent His Son into the world to tell us of His Love for us!

Narrator: May we take the angels' message to all the world! In a world where there is so much fear, we say, like the angels, "Do not be afraid! We have Good News — the Savior of the World has been born!"

These people are very much like us…

The Three Kings were very persistent — they traveled for a long time through unfamiliar lands to look upon the face of Jesus. *(We too travel every day — to school, to work, to run errands — do we look to find Jesus in the faces of each person we meet?)*

The Angels sang to the shepherds about the birth of Jesus — they brought GOOD NEWS to the world. *(Do we bring Good News to all we meet — how can we be more like angles telling other people about the joy of loving Jesus?)*

Now, we ask you to think about these things — as we make our craft about the Journey to the Light of Jesus.

Advent Wheel Craft:

Supplies for Advent Wheel Craft

- Large round pizza cardboards, covered in dark construction paper, with the words "Journey to the Light of Jesus"
- A "baggie" for each family with a manger (small cardstock square covered with hay) and black line outlines of Mary, Joseph, a shepherd with sheep, the Three Kings holding gifts, a donkey or cow, a star, and an angel.

Provide the following items in a separate "baggie" to be used to "fill in" the figures on the Advent Wheel

- Light blue scraps of construction paper or material — Mary
- Small pieces of black, brown, and tan construction paper to fill in the animals
- Short pieces of black or brown yarn for the animal tails
- Googly eyes for the animals
- Straw or raffia to glue on the manger
- Circle for Jesus' head with halo drawn in gold marker
- Soft material scraps for the manger blanket
- Gold glitter for the star
- Burlap or brown cloth scraps for Joseph
- Brown pipe cleaner for the shepherd staff
- Small foam heart for the shepherd
- Cotton balls and a googly eye for the sheep
- Silver or gold decorating twine — or ribbon — for the angel halo
- Star sticker for the Three Kings to follow
- Bright pieces of red or purple material scraps or ribbon for the Kings' clothing
- Whole cloves and a gold ribbon piece for the Kings' gifts
- Glue and glue applicators

(All figures on the Advent Wheel are not covered entirely; the above items are simply glued on part of the figure as the child wishes. Encourage the children to place a small picture of themselves on the "Journey to the Light of Jesus" when they get home.)

Preparation Ahead of Time for Advent Wheel Craft

1. Make the baggies with the above supplies — or if the number of families is not large, simply put all the items on the tables.
2. Cover the pizza cardboards with dark paper as a contrast to the items being placed on the wheels.
3. Glue the "Journey to the Light of Jesus" border on the cardboard wheels.

It is recommended that the glitter and straw are done at a different table due to the messiness involved!

Journey to the Light of Jesus

Advent Candle Craft (if desired):

Supplies

- 8-ounce clear plastic cup filled with uncooked popcorn, cranberries, or dry beans
- 3 ounces of white glue (the kind that dries clear) per candle
- "Emergency" candles — the 6" type

Directions

Pour 3 ounces of white glue (the kind that dries clear) over an 8-ounce clear plastic cup of popcorn kernels, cranberries, or dry beans

Stick a candle in the middle

When the glue dries completely (in a few days), the candleholder can be simply pulled out of the plastic cup.

Refreshments:

Christmas cookies, punch, and coffee

Project Checklist

3. THE WORD OF GOD

Objective:

To review with the families familiar stories from the Hebrew and New Testaments, and to reveal the importance of the Bible in our worship and in our daily lives.

Setting:

On the center of each table where the families will be sitting, there is a wrapped Bible. The Bibles are wrapped in either brown paper, gold paper, comic strip paper, or white paper. Inside the Bibles are pictures or clues of items to be used in the activity as the stories are being narrated. There is a backdrop running along the wall comprised of black paper; a mountain sketch with the figure of Abraham, his three visitors, and his tent; a rainbow; a coloring book outline of a pillar of fire and a pillar of clouds; and a crown. These symbols represent the Hebrew Scripture stories of Creation; Abraham; Noah; the desert journey of Moses and the Israelites; and the reign of Solomon. There is a simple manger (real or a picture) scene to end the backdrop. A figure of "Moses," the Ten Commandments, and an "ark" are elsewhere in the room. The refreshment table is covered until after the activity.

Activity Summary:

After greeting the families, the Narrator directs the families to unwrap the Bibles, explaining the significance of each of the four colors of wrapping paper. Then the children listen to the summary of each story, and come forward to place the appropriate pictures found in their Bibles on the backdrop. The Hebrew Testament stories end with the Nativity scene — at which time, a simple play follows with the actors of Jesus and the two disciples. The disciples gather the children around Jesus, and he performs two miracles and tells the children a parable. After the play, all share hospitality. Families are invited to make a "Shema Prayer Scroll."

Items Needed for the Bible Activity:

- Bibles for each table — evenly wrapped in either brown, gold, comic, or white paper
- Pictures of animals, people, trees, stars (creation)
- Abraham's twelve sons (comic book figures cut out and colored)
- Cardboard ark (cardboard with black lines shaped like an ark)
- Moses figure
- Ten Commandments (list or scroll)
- Yellow flames
- Cloud pictures

The Word of God

- Picture of the Temple (enlarge one found in a book, or on the Internet)
- Tape
- Manger with straw (a star behind it works well!)
- Doll (representing Jesus)

Abraham and the three visitors

Abraham's Sons: Four Brothers (make three copies and color distinctively to make twelve.)

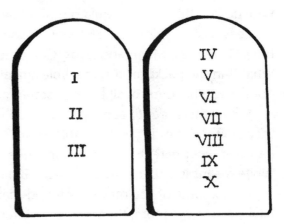

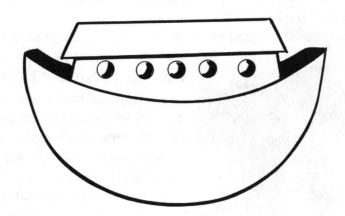

Bible Activity Script:

Today, we are learning about the Bible — the Word of God. Let's look at your tables — how many of you have a brown package in the middle of your table? Brown means OLD — it means something that has a long history, something that has been around "forever." Unwrap it — see what it is? It is a Bible. The Bible has been around for thousands of years — a thousand years before Jesus was even born! That is why we wrapped it in brown to help you remember how old the Bible is.

I see other packages in the middle of your tables — I see GOLD paper — Gold means something very expensive, very precious — very important. Unwrap it now and see what it is. Why do you think we put gold on this Bible? Because the Bible is SO VALUABLE! It is a treasure!

Let's see — I think I see cartoons on some tables. What is that? Are there people on the pictures — families, Moms and Dads, Grandmothers and Grandfathers — on your comic strips? What is in the package? It is the Bible again! Does the Bible tell stories about people? Yes, it does! The Bible is full of all types of stories about people's lives.

I think there are still some packages on some tables that haven't been unwrapped — are they white? What do you think this means? White means clean — pure — like when you were baptized, your parents placed you in white clothing. Maybe you have seen pictures of that. White means it is special to God — the Bible is God's Word!

I think some of you may have found that inside your Bible are pictures, or maybe clues. Look around the room, there are some interesting things on the wall behind me — and in other parts of the room here.

This is a time line behind me — a time line of the Old Testament. (Hold up Bible.) This is the part of the Bible that Jesus knew when He was a little boy — it was the history of Jesus' family. Stories that are part of our family history too, stories that Jesus knew so well from hearing them as a child. Stories of the Old Testament — we hear one reading from the Old Testament when we go to Mass each week.

Let's open the Bible and see if there are things in it to help us learn about these stories. Just like in our lives, the Bible gives us answers to our questions.

Our first story is when God created the earth — He created the sun, moon, stars, water, animals, flowers — everything on Earth God created, and God called all His creations GOOD. Do some of you have pictures of God's creations in your Bibles? Please bring them up and put them on this black part of our backdrop.

Our next story from the Old Testament is about Abraham. Abraham was chosen by God for

Sample picture of Abraham's tent

a special purpose! He was told by God that he would be the Father of a great number of people — the Father of many nations — his family would outnumber the stars! Does anyone have pictures of Abraham's sons, in their Bibles?

We have all heard of Noah — the kind and honest man whom God the Father chose to build an ark and take two animals of every kind and keep them safe during a flood on Earth. There is a large ark in the room. I think in someone's Bible

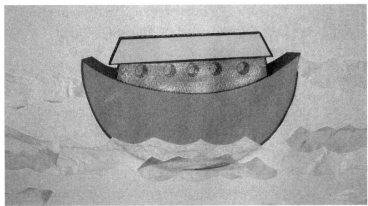

Sample pictures of ark and rainbow

there is a clue about where to find the ark. We are going to place the ark next to the rainbow. Remember, after the flood, God said He would never flood the earth again — and He sent a rainbow to remind us of that promise.

Then the Old Testament continues with the story of Moses — Moses, the leader of the Jewish people, who led them from slavery to freedom over forty years walking in the desert. Does anyone have a clue in their Bible to tell us where Moses can be found? Please bring him up. The Bible tells us that God led Moses by a cloud cover during the day and by fire in the cloud at night so that people could see their way. Please find the pictures of clouds and fire — and come up to fill in the outline.

God also chose Moses to give the Ten Commandments. These are rules the Jewish people and Jesus lived by — and we as Catholics live by today. Please bring up the list of the Ten Commandments and tape them on the figure of Moses.

Example of a Moses puppet, costume, or illustration and pillars of clouds and fire

The Word of God

Sample picture of crown

When the Jewish people settled in the holy land, they were ruled by kings. One king — Solomon — asked God to give him wisdom to lead his people. God answered Solomon's prayer and blessed him with a wonderfully understanding heart and mind to judge right and wrong. In gratitude to God, Solomon built a magnificent temple to worship Him. Where can we find the temple to bring up?

Jesus knew all these stories, they were part of His life. Like your parents may read you stories at night before bed, or in the afternoon, Jesus' Mother Mary, or Joseph, her husband, did the same for Jesus.

What happened next? We have gone through some important stories of the Old Testament, there are many more.

Now look — we have these items here — a manger, with straw — it must be a stable — oh, there is a baby inside. What happened in our history — told in the Bible now? This represents the birth of Jesus — we are now in the part of the Bible called the New Testament. We hear two readings from the New Testament each time we go to Mass. (Hold up the Bible and show how much of the Bible is the New Testament compared to the Old Testament/Hebrew Scriptures.)

Now Jesus grew in wisdom, through prayer and reading the Scriptures, and He learned about God and the messages that God has for our lives. Then He became a man — and He gathered His friends who were fishermen. He said they would become "fishers of men."

A real manger can be used or glue some straw onto a picture like this one.

Actors for the Play:
Jesus
Two disciples
Blind man
Child with the bread and fish to offer

Props for Play:
- Simple costumes for the actors
- Fishing net (if desired)
- Construction paper for "loaves and fish"
- Two baskets, with paper cover over cut-up bread inside the baskets
- Large basket to cover up the "light"
- Light (battery candle)
- Bowl of water (if desired) for the blind man
- Clay (if desired) to put on the blind man

(PLAY BEGINS)
Jesus walks up from a back (hidden) area — and calls the fishermen (two disciples are sitting as if repairing a net) to follow Him.

Jesus: "Fishermen, come follow Me — I will make you fishers of men!"

Narrator: Many people, families with children, people of all ages, followed Jesus amazed at all He had to say. He was so kind and loving to all who met Him.

(The two disciples invite all the children to come and sit down around the floor at the feet of Jesus.)

Narrator: Jesus performed many miracles. *(A blind man — wearing a blindfold — walks in, feeling his way, stumbling or bumping into an obstacle. Jesus gets up and walks over to him.)*

Narrator: This man had been blind from birth. Imagine never being able to see the faces of people you love, or a flower, or anything around you!

(The disciples reach out to him, but he doesn't see them, and walks on, feeling the air in front of him.)

Narrator: But then something special happened, Jesus came into his life. Jesus did something strange, He spit on the dirt and made some mud. Then He put the mud on the man's eyes. *(Jesus leans down and with pretend spit and clay — rubs this on the man's eyes.)*

Narrator: "Go and wash your eyes." Jesus said.

The blind man goes over to a nearby bowl of water and washes his eyes — opens them in great excitement and says…

Blind Man: "I can see! Thank you Jesus, I can see!"

Narrator: The man did what Jesus said — he washed the mud off his eyes, looked around, and could see! The man was so happy and worshipped Jesus!

The Word of God

Narrator: Jesus also fed a large crowd of over 5,000 people who were hungry after traveling all day to come and listen to Him. When Jesus noticed the people were hungry, a small boy came forward with five small loaves of bread and two fish. Jesus took the boy's offering and held it up for God to bless. Jesus than gave baskets of bread and fish to His disciples to pass out to all the hungry people. After everyone was fed, there was still food left over!

(Following the script, a small child comes up and gives Jesus bread and fish. Jesus smiles and takes it from him, puts them in two baskets, holds them up to God in prayer, then gives them to His two disciples. The disciples break through the thin paper in the baskets, uncovering pieces of cut-up bread, and go through the crowd of children giving bread to everyone.)

Narrator: He told many stories that were about things in nature — things that were part of everyday life — such as water, seeds, and light. Let's listen to what Jesus said about light.

(With props of a candle and a bushel basket, Jesus reads the gospel.)

Jesus: "No one after lighting a lamp covers it with a vessel or puts under a bed, but puts it on a stand, that those who enter may see the light" (Luke 8:16). You, boys and girls, are the light of the world! Let your light shine so that everyone may see your good deeds and thank God your Father in Heaven!

Narrator: The most important teaching of Jesus was about Love — how we are to love and care for each other. Jesus loved children. No matter how tired He was, He wanted the children to sit at His side. They were so important to Him — just like you are today. Jesus loves you just as He loved the children in His days on Earth.

Jesus stands up, smiles and touches the children around him.

Narrator: These are the stories we hear in Mass every week. The importance of all that happened before Jesus, about how God loved and saved His people — and about Jesus, His teachings, and His love for us.

The Bible tells us how to live like Jesus. Let us leave here today, promising Jesus that we will listen always to what God tells us through the readings.

"Shema Prayer Scroll" Craft Activity:

Supplies
(per scroll)
- Rectangles of "Parchment" paper (if available, or any paper will do) with prayer printed in center (see next page)
- Two 6" round craft sticks
- Tape

Directions
Tape sticks on both ends of paper.
Roll toward center to make scroll.

Refreshments:
Anything is suitable!

"Hear, O Israel! The Lord your God

Is One.

And you shall love Him with all

Your heart,

With all your soul,

With all your strength,

And with all your mind."

"Hear, O Israel! The Lord your God

Is One.

And you shall love Him with all

Your heart,

With all your soul,

With all your strength,

And with all your mind."

"Hear, O Israel! The Lord your God

Is One.

And you shall love Him with all

Your heart,

With all your soul,

With all your strength,

And with all your mind."

"Hear, O Israel! The Lord your God

Is One.

And you shall love Him with all

Your heart,

With all your soul,

With all your strength,

And with all your mind."

4. THE LITURGY OF THE EUCHARIST

Objective:

Preferably held around Thanksgiving, this Family Gathering connects the term "Eucharist" with the holiday of Thanksgiving and focuses the families on their blessings completed by the greatest blessing of all — The Gift of Jesus in the Eucharist.

Setting:

On the center wall behind the seated group of families is a very large sign reading EUCHARIST = THANKSGIVING = BLESSINGS. Under the BLESSINGS area on the wall are smaller signs reading "People Who Take Care of Me"; "Play and Fun"; "Places to Learn"; "Things We Need"; "Beautiful Things"; and "Friends."

Above the BLESSINGS sign is a rolled up sketch of a picture of Jesus with His arms out-stretched holding up the chalice and host. On the tables where the families are sitting are pieces of gold wrapping paper and markers/pencils.

Activity Summary:

After the families are seated at their tables, the Narrator begins by briefly explaining that the second part of the Mass is called the "Liturgy of the Eucharist" — the part of the Mass when Jesus comes to us under the forms of bread and wine. Then the narration continues with tying in simple meal prayers like we say at home, and the Eucharistic prayers spoken by the priest. A volunteer parent or older child comes up and reads a sample "meal grace" from the center of their table. These meal prayers are written on a sketch of a dinner table. On the reverse side of the paper is a simple sketch of an altar with similar words of the Eucharistic prayers written on it. The Narrator ties in the similarity of the two prayers. The Narrator continues explaining that the word EUCHARIST in Greek means the word THANKSGIVING, and that THANKSGIVING is a time when we remember all our blessings. Families are

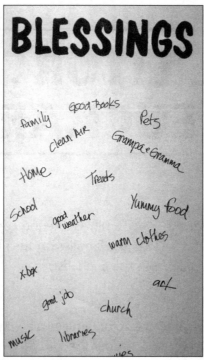

invited to come forward and write their blessings on the categories listed. After a few minutes, the Narrator reads some of the blessings listed. After this discussion, the picture of Jesus is unfurled, and it now covers the various lists of blessings. (Preferably the sketch is done on fairly thin paper so that the blessings can be read through it.) The Narrator explains that all our blessings are given by God, and the Gift of Jesus is the greatest blessing of our lives. The Narrator explains that when the bread and wine are brought up and given to the priest at Mass, it means each of us offers ourselves to God, and we become part of the Body of Christ. The families at the tables are now invited to take a piece of gold wrapping paper and write their names (or draw their picture) and take them up to the wall and fill in the outlines of the chalice. Helpers are at the wall to assist taping in the large outline. Then the families move to stand in a large circle on the floor. When everyone is done, and the circle is complete, the Narrator explains that this circle is like the Host — all of us together make the Body of Christ. The Narrator explains that as a circle never ends, Jesus' love for us and the blessings He gives never end either. As the Body of Christ we pray for each other and see each of us as a blessing to the others. A designated person walks around the circle with the families giving their names, and the group responds: "May God bless and keep the _____ family." Families go back to their tables and outline their hands on various colors of construction paper. These hands are glued together on cardboard to form a wreath. The families then write on the wreath the blessings they had previously written — or the blessings others had written. As the families leave, they are given a small "Meal Prayer" booklet with prayers from a variety of cultures and ethnic groups — to symbolize the Body of Christ.

Script Supplies:
- Large signs reading EUCHARIST = THANKSGIVING = BLESSINGS
- Outline of large chalice (use page 33 and enlarge with overhead and outline)
- Large sheet of white paper with the headings: People Who Take Care of Me; Play and Fun; Things We Need; Places to Learn; Beautiful Things; and Friends
- Markers
- Small pieces of gold wrapping paper
- Tape

- Large outline or picture of Jesus (use page 33 and enlarge with overhead and outline)
- Table and Eucharistic/Altar Prayers — included. Photocopy so that the Table Prayer is on the front of the sheet and the Eucharistic Prayer on the back (be sure to match them up according to the letter assigned to each one)
- Meal Prayers — included

Script:

Thanks for joining us for our Family Gathering today!

Remember the Family Gathering when we talked about all the Bible stories — the Bible stories we hear during the first part of the Mass? We hear stories about what Jesus did and what He said. This is the *Liturgy of the Word.*

The second part of the Mass is called the *Liturgy of the Eucharist.* What do you think the word EUCHARIST means? It is a Greek word meaning THANKSGIVING! That is why we have equal signs up here on the wall. What does Thanksgiving mean to us? A time to count our blessings; a time to thank God for our food at the dinner table. *Think of this part of the Mass as when you say grace at the dinner table before you eat.*

When Father says his prayers at the altar during the Mass, they are very much like the meal prayers or grace that you say at home.

Let's see how similar the prayers are: You have sheets of papers on the tables. One side has a meal grace like you say at home and it is written on a dining room table; on the other side is an altar, like the one we have in Church. On this altar are the actual words that Father says when he prays before Communion.

We'd like a volunteer to please come up and read the grace from the "dining room table" and then turn the page over and read the Eucharistic Prayer from the "altar table." Remember these words are the words Father prays when he stands behind the altar, right before everyone comes up to receive Communion. They are prayers of THANKSGIVING for God's gift of the bread and wine — and for God's many blessings that He gives to us each day. What words do you find that are alike? On your tables, we have other examples of meal prayers and Eucharistic prayers — take a few minutes and talk about them at your table.

We would like you now to talk about all the blessings you have in your lives. There are hints on the paper up here: "People Who Take Care of Me"; "Play and Fun"; "Places to Learn"; "Things We Need"; "Beautiful Things"; and "Friends." Please come up to the paper and write down the blessings you have thought about. *(After the families are done…)* Let's read some of the blessings that you have written.

Boys and girls, who gave us all of these good things? Yes, all our blessings come from God Who Loves us and takes care of all our needs. God sent Jesus to teach us about love. Jesus is God's greatest blessing to us! What is so special is that Jesus is always with us. He is with us when we pray, when we read the Bible, when we are kind to each other — and most especially Jesus is with us in Communion, in the Eucharist!

Remember at Mass when two people carry up the bread and wine? It means that they give themselves as an offering to God. They represent everyone in the whole Church! We all become the Body of Christ. We all offer ourselves to God every time we go to Mass. We are all connected because we all love Jesus. When we receive Communion, we become more like Jesus.

The Liturgy of the Eucharist

To help us remember that we all are ONE in the Body of Christ, we would like you to write your family name or draw your family on the gold paper then come up and fill in the chalice. When you are done, please form a circle in the open space — one big circle.

(After the families have finished taping their names on the chalice, they join and form one large circle.)

A circle is important because it doesn't have a beginning or an end — just like God's love and His blessings never end, but just keep going. This circle, too, is like the Host — the communion bread — we receive at Mass. All of us here are the Body of Christ, and since we are all connected, we need to pray for each other.

Let's go around the circle — just say your family name, and all of us will say together: "May God bless and keep the _____ family."

(After the blessings of the families…)

Our craft will help you remember what we did today. We ask for the parents to trace and cut out the pattern of your children's hands and make a small wreath from them. Then write down on the wreath the blessings you wrote up here on our list on the wall. We have tiny clothespins for you to stick on too — you can use them to put notes on your wreath for special things you want to thank God for.

Giving Thanks Blessings Booklet

Copy pages 46-50. Cut the pages in half on the dotted lines, hole punch, and attach together with yarn, string, or paper fasteners

Thanksgiving Wreath Craft:

Supplies

- Variety of colored construction paper
- Scissors
- Small cardboard wreaths
- Glue and applicator sticks
- If available (in craft or "dollar" stores) tiny clothespins

Directions

Trace the children's hands on a variety of colored construction paper.

Cut them out.

Glue them overlapping to cover the small cardboard wreath.

Write down the blessings on the wreath that the family members had written on the wall display.

Glue (if available) the tiny clothespins to hold future notes of blessings received.

Refreshments:

A variety of types of bread, butter, and jam
Grape juice

Chalice and Jesus templates — enlarge and trace on an overhead

A

Table Prayer
We thank You, Heavenly Father,
for every earthly good:
For health, happiness, and family,
and for our daily food. Amen.

B

Table Prayer

Our Heavenly Father, kind and good,
we thank You for our daily food.
We thank You for Your love and care.
Be with us, Lord, and hear our prayer.
Amen.

C

Table Prayer

Father, thank You for allowing us to share this meal together.
Send Your Spirit to bless these gifts which You give us.
We thank You for our food and ALL Your blessings,
in the name of Your Son, Jesus Christ.
Amen.

D

Table Prayer
Our Father in Heaven, for this meal You have given,
we want to say thank You from our hearts.
Bless the ones who prepared it,
and Lord, as we share it — will You stay with us and be our guest of honor.

E

Table Prayer

The Lord is good to me
and so I thank the Lord
for giving me the things I need,
the sun and the rain and the apple seed.
The Lord is good to me.

F

Table Prayer

Bless us, O Lord, and this food to our use
and keep us ever mindful of the needs of others.
We especially pray for those whom we love
who are far away from our table tonight.
Amen.

A

Eucharistic Prayer for Children

God, our Father, You have brought us here together so that we can give You thanks and praise for all the wonderful things You have done. We thank You for all that is beautiful in the world and for the happiness You have given us. We praise You for the earth and for all the people who live on it, and for our life which comes from You.

B

Eucharistic Prayer for Children

Yes, Lord, You are holy:

You are kind to us and to all.

For this we thank You.

We thank You, above all, for Your Son, Jesus Christ

C

Eucharistic Prayer
Lord, our God, listen to our prayer.
Send the Holy Spirit to all of us who share in this meal.
May this Spirit bring us closer together in the family of the Church.

D

Eucharistic Prayer

You have gathered us here around the table of Your Son,
in fellowship with the Virgin Mary, Mother of God, and all the saints,
with Jesus Christ, the Lord.

E

Eucharistic Prayer
Because You love us,
You gave us this great and beautiful world.
With Jesus we sing Your praises!

F

Eucharistic Prayer

Father, because You love us, You invite us to come to Your table.
Lord, You never forget any of Your children.
We ask You to take care of Your children, especially _____ and _____ ,
and we pray for those who have died.

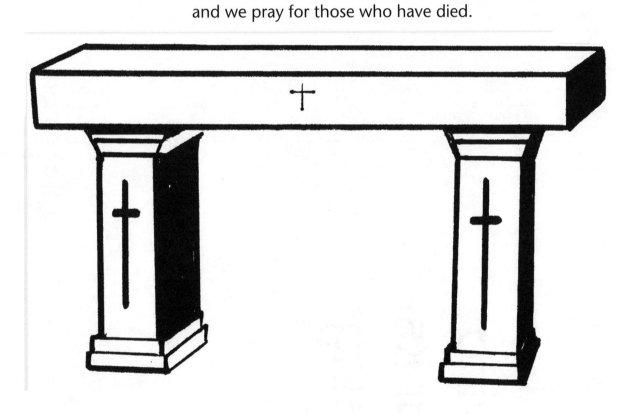

Bless us, O Lord,
and these thy gifts,
which we are about to receive
from thy bounty.
Through Christ Our Lord.
Amen.

For each new morning with its light,
for rest and shelter of the night,
for health and food,
for love and friends,
for everything
Thy goodness sends.

— Emerson

Giving
Thanks
Blessings

For food that stays our hunger,
for rest that brings us ease,
for homes where memories linger,
we give our thanks for these.

The Lord bless you and keep you;
the Lord make his face shine upon you
and be gracious to you.
The Lord turn his face toward you
and give you peace.

— Irish

May the Warm Winds of Heaven blow softly
upon your house. May the Great Spirit bless
all who enter there. May your moccasins make
happy tracks in many snows, and may the
rainbow always touch your shoulder.

— Cherokee

Come, Lord Jesus, our guest to be
and bless these gifts bestowed by Thee.
And bless our loved ones everywhere,
and keep them in your loving care.

Holy Father,
give us each a thankful mind:
make us more
like Jesus,
gentle, pure, and kind.

— Parker

• • • • • • • • • • • •

God bless this food,
that it may make my body strong and free.
God bless my life
that I may know the joy of serving Thee.

For health to be hungry,
for food every day,
for hands that have served it,
we thank Jesus today.

• • • • • • • • • • •

For all of our family, thank you, God.
For all that we eat, thank you, God.
For the birds and the trees
and the sound of the leaves,
for all that we have, thank you, God.

Bless me, Lord, from head to feet.
Now bless this food we're about to eat.
O You who feed the little birds,
bless our food, O Lord.
O God, make us thankful for all that's
on the table.

For health and food,
for love and friends,
for everything Your goodness sends,
Father in Heaven, we thank You.
Amen.

Thank you for the world so sweet,
Thank you for the food we eat.
Thank you for the birds that sing.
Thank you, God, for everything.

Enter His gates with thanksgiving.
Enter His courts with praise.
Give thanks to Him, bless His name.

— From Psalm 100

Bless this meal we share.
Grace us with your presence and
be a guest at our table.
Thank you for our life together.
Amen.

How wonderful, O Lord, are the
works of Your hands!
The heavens declare Your glory.
In Your love You have given us the
power to behold the beauty
of Your world.

When you arise in the morning,
give thanks for the morning light,
for your life and strength.
Give thanks for your food
and the joy of living.

We bless Your presence in our lives
and in our hearts!
Take of this offering to Your delight,
and be filled with prayers of thanksgiving!
— African

5. PRAYER

Objective:

To help children and their parents learn about various forms of prayer and provide them with a take-home craft to encourage daily prayer at home.

Setting:

The tables where the families will sit have several wooden blocks with pictures of saints taped on them. They also may have a large balloon with the word "BIG" on it and a barely inflated balloon taped with the word "small." If other examples of objects in both very LARGE and very small sizes are available, these objects may be on tables as well. Each table has a small ball of yarn, and one table or two may have some form of "turkey/Thanksgiving" decoration. The craft and refreshment tables remain covered until after the presentation.

Activity Summary:

The families engage with each other in activities at the table focusing on "Large and Small Prayers"; the Sign of the Cross; Prayers of Thanksgiving; Intercessory Prayers; Prayers of Petition; and Blessings. After the blessings of parent to child and child to parent, an explanation of the two crafts follow, and all enjoy refreshments while participating in the crafts. As the families leave, they are given handouts with an explanation of the activities to remind them of the various forms of prayer that were presented and a child's page of "Five Finger Prayers."

Script:

Welcome everyone to our Family Gathering! Our focus today is on PRAYER.

We'll be doing a few activities at our tables together, and then we have two craft projects for you to take home today to help you remember what we have talked about this morning. We also have some important papers to give to each of you today at the end of our time.

Prayer is when we talk to God and listen to what He says to us.

Our prayers may be very big or very simple — it doesn't matter to God — He listens to us every time we pray — whether our prayers are BIG (like for peace in the world) or small (like we want a sunny day to play outside). What are some other examples you can think of for very big prayers — or for small ones as well?

Let's begin with a prayer we are all familiar with — we pray it with our bodies. We move our hands to say the prayer called the Sign of the Cross.

We do this often — when we enter or leave the Church and sign ourselves with holy water; when we pray during the Mass; at baptisms; when we receive communion; when we see the priest to make our confession. What are some other times we make the Sign of the Cross? Some families make the Sign of the Cross when they say grace at meals, or before bed.

Let's say it together: In the name of the Father, Son, and Holy Spirit. Amen.

When we make this sign — by touching our heads, shoulders, and heart — we give ourselves to God. <u>We are saying that we belong to God, that He is our Father and will take care of us because He loves us.</u> Let's move our hands with the motions of the Sign of the Cross, and say, "We — belong — to — God."

Now — I see a few turkeys on the tables. What does this mean to you? It reminds us of Thanksgiving. Thanksgiving is another form of prayer we use in Church, at home, and in our private prayers with Jesus. When we say: Thank you, God, for my home, my family, my grade on a test. What are some other things we thank God for?

Let's practice. Who would like to come up and say what they are thankful for?

The rest of us will say: Thanks be to God.

There is another form of prayer that is very important. It is when we ask our saints, or our own loved ones who are in Heaven with Jesus, to pray for us.

You have blocks on your tables. I see some of them have pictures of saints on them, or words.

We believe that when we need God's help we can ask the people in Heaven to pray for us. We call this <u>intercessory prayer.</u>

Let's see how this works: Could I have a volunteer come up and tell us what they need help praying for?

(Example): Please, God, help my Grandma feel better.

What we can do now is to ask Mary, the Mother of Jesus to pray for us by saying, "Mary, please pray to Jesus for my Grandma."

Or Saint Patrick — or any of the saints and angels in Heaven — they will pray for what we need. Also, if you have loved ones who have already gone to Heaven to be with Jesus, ask them to pray to Jesus for you. Please bring up the blocks from your tables, and we will build our prayer up to Heaven. The blocks are building up to Heaven — our prayers are rising and are joined by the saints and our loved ones.

Now, we have another type of prayer that you will recognize from church. When the Lector says a special intention like, "Let us pray for the sick of our parish family," and we say, "Lord hear our prayer." These are prayers of petition.

Let's try that at our tables — when we pray for each other and we say "Lord hear our prayer," we are all joined together as one family.

We would like you to share a prayer, say together "Lord hear our prayer," and place the yarn around your wrist, then throw the ball of yarn to someone else at your table.

When everyone has had a chance to pray, we see by the yarn that you are all tied together in a very special way.

Another type of prayer is a blessing. We pray by asking God to bless someone else.

We ask parents now to make the Sign of the Cross on your child's forehead and say: "May God bless you and keep you in His loving arms."

Children's blessings are very important too!

We would like the children to bless their Moms and Dads.

Boys and girls, take your Mom's hand and make the Sign of the Cross and say, "May God bless and guide you as my Mom." Then take your Dad's hand and say, "May God bless and guide you as my Dad."

Now we have learned about the Sign of the Cross, when we say, "We — belong — to — God"; and prayers of thanksgiving, when we say, "Thanks be to God"; and intercessory prayers, when the angels and saints pray for us and our prayers build up toward Heaven; and prayers of petition, when we pray for each other and say, "Lord hear our prayer" and become one family; and prayers of blessing.

What happens in all these types of prayers is that we change — prayer changes us!

Our crafts today will help you see that: *(Hold up example of the craft.)*

As you can see by our *"Don't Be a Dud Spud!"* prayer changes how we see the world and everyone around us — and it changes us inside too!

Prayer gives us <u>new eyes</u> so we know to make good choices, and how to see the needs of others around us.

Prayer gives us <u>new ears</u> to hear God speaking to us in the Bible and in the words of our parents and teachers.

Prayer gives us <u>love in our heart to share</u> with others and <u>hands and feet to do the work of Jesus and to follow Him.</u>

We have everything for you to make this to take home. We even have a few potatoes here if you would rather have a real "potato head" rather than the picture.

Also, we have a Prayer Pocket for you to put your prayers in — it will help you to remember to pray and help you to know that God answers prayers.

On the craft table are pieces of material and pockets to glue together, and we have baskets of sample prayers for you to take home to get you started.

Our take-home papers will help you remember all the types of prayers that we talked about. And we have a list of "Five Finger Prayers" — all you have to do to pray is move your fingers! God loves you, and He loves it when we pray — remember really big prayers and simple little prayers are all the same.

Script Supplies:
- Wooden blocks with pictures of saints taped on them — may also add some blocks with the names Grandma, Grandfather, Neighbor, Aunt, etc.
- Small balls of yarn (one for each table)
- Large and small objects of like kind — (balloons, etc.)
- Thanksgiving decoration of turkey, etc.

Prayer

Crafts Supplies and Directions:

Prayer Changes Us "Spud" Craft

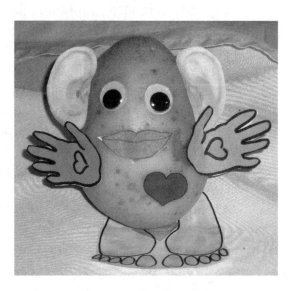

Supplies
- Template of potato
- A few washed potatoes (if desired)
- Googly eyes
- Cutout ears, mouth, heart, feet, and hands (see page 55)

Directions
Potato Body — real potato or construction paper.
Add EYES.
Add EARS.
Add a HEART.
Add HANDS.
Add FEET.

Prayer Pocket Craft

Supplies
- 12" x 12" pieces of material — the top hemmed to hold a dowel if desired
- 4" to 16" thin wooden dowels
- Yarn to tie on the Prayer Pocket in order to hang it
- 4" x 3" cut material
- Fabric glue and sticks to apply it
- Cut up sample prayers (see pages 58–59)

Directions
Glue the pockets as desired on the material.
Place dowel in the hemmed top.
Tie yarn at both ends of the dowel to hang.
Select prayers to put in the pockets.

Refreshments:
Variety of cut-up fruit with the sign: "Prayer Produces Good Fruit!"

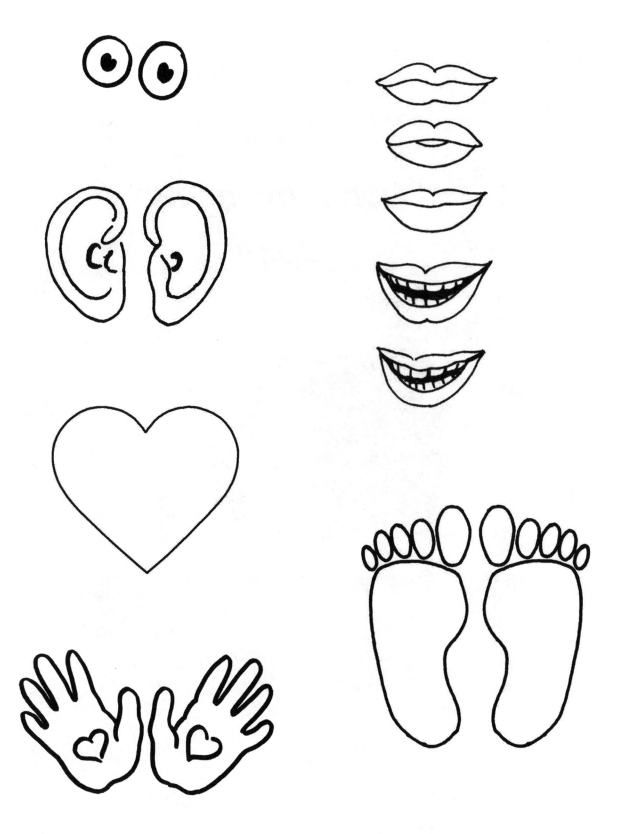

Spud craft templates

Finished craft sample

Don't be a dud spud!

Let prayer add some SENSE to your life:

God be in my EYES so I see good choices.

God be in my EARS so I hear the word of God.

God be in my HEART so I share His love with others.

God be in my HANDS so I do Jesus' work on earth.

God be in my FEET so I will follow Him all my life.

Trinity Prayer

Love of Jesus

Fill us.

Holy Spirit

Guide us.

Will of the Father

be done.

Amen.

Praise God,

from whom all

blessings flow;

Praise Him,

all creatures here below;

Praise Him above,

ye heavenly host;

Praise Father,

Son, and Holy Ghost.

Good Morning, God

You are ushering in another

day

untouched and freshly new

so here I come to ask You,

God,

if You'll renew me, too,

forgive the many errors

that I made yesterday

and let me try again, dear

God,

to walk closer in thy way.

Hail Mary, full of grace,

The Lord is with thee.

Blessed art thou among

women

and blessed is the fruit

of thy womb, Jesus.

Holy Mary, Mother of God,

pray for us sinners,

now, and at the hour

of our death.

Amen.

Two little eyes

to look at God.

Two little ears

to hear His word.

Two little lips

to sing His praise.

Two little feet

to walk His ways.

Two little hands

to do His will.

One little heart

to love Him still.

We Come to You in Prayer

Dear Lord, we come to you

in prayer,

knowing You are always there.

Joyfully, your songs we sing,

praising You in everything.

Keep us safe by night and day,

as we travel on our way.

Teach us that its when we

share,

others learn about your care.

Forgive me, Lord,

for this I pray,

the wrong that I have

done this day.

May peace with God

and neighbor be,

before I sleep,

restored to me.

God be in my head

and in my understanding.

God be my eyes

and in my looking.

God be in my mouth

and in my speaking.

God be in my heart

and in my thinking.

Our Father, Who art in Heaven,
Hallowed be Thy Name.
Thy kingdom come.
Thy will be done.
On earth as it is in Heaven.
Give us this day,
our daily bread,
and forgive us our trespasses,
as we forgive those who
trespass against us.
And lead us not
into temptation,
but deliver us from evil. Amen.

May you walk in Peace,
live with Love,
work with Joy,
and may God go with you.

I see the moon,
and the moon sees me.
God bless the moon,
and God bless me.

But, Father, I am well aware
I can't make it on my own.
So take my hand and
hold it tight
for I can't walk alone!

Good morning, dear God,
I offer to You
my thoughts,
words, and actions
and all that I do.
Amen.

Glory be to the Father,
to the Son,
and to the Holy Spirit.
As it was in the beginning,
is now and ever shall be,
world without end.
Amen.

Thank You, Lord,
for food and clothes and toys
    and such,
we thank you, Lord, so very much.
And when it's time for us to sleep,
we ask you, Lord, our souls
    to keep.

Jesus, Savior,
    wash away all
    that has been wrong today.
    Help us every day to be good
    and gentle,
    more like Thee.

Five Fingers Prayer

Just five words long, these little prayers are good for reminding us of God's loving presence in times of stress or worry. Tap each finger as you say the word and remember He is always by our side.

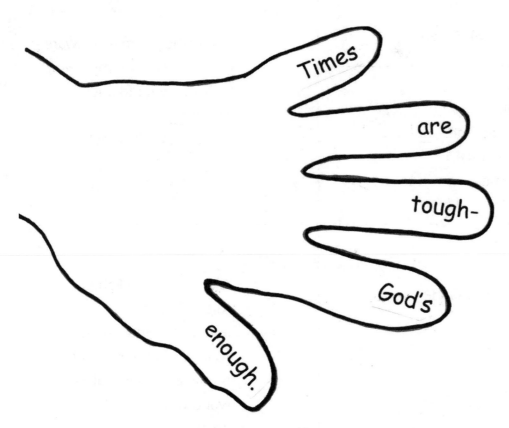

Here are some more:

"This, too, is from me."
"Let me look after you."
"Feeling down? Try looking up."
"I am with you always."
"Love ALL God's many children."

What I learned today about my prayers...

The Sign of the Cross (*when we touch our head, heart, and shoulders and say: "In the Name of the Father, Son, and Holy Spirit, Amen"*) helps us to remember that we belong to God. He is our Father and will always take care of us because He loves us.

Thanksgiving Prayers are when we thank God for all He gives us and does for us and for those we love. We say, "Thanks be to God!"

Intercessory Prayers are when we ask the saints, angels, and our loved ones in heaven with Jesus to pray for us. Their prayers join us in reaching up to Heaven. "Holy Mary, Mother of God, please pray for us."

Prayers of Petition are when we say a prayer with others in Church or at home, and we say, "Lord, hear our prayer." These prayers remind us that we are all one family praying for the needs of ourselves and others.

Blessings are prayers when we ask God to bless someone we love in a special way. Today our parents blessed us by saying: "May God bless you and keep you in His loving arms."

We blessed our moms and dads by saying: "May God bless and guide you as my mom and dad."

And we remember:

PRAYER CHANGES US!
ALL PRAYERS — LARGE, SMALL — ARE ALIKE TO GOD!
HE LISTENS AND HE LOVES US!

Project Checklist

_____
_____
_____
_____
_____
_____
_____
_____
_____
_____
_____
_____
_____
_____
_____
_____
_____
_____
_____
_____
_____

6. Stewardship — Taking Care of All God's Gifts

Objective:

To help children and their families gain an understanding of actions and attitudes that reflects a reverence for all God's Gifts.

Setting:

The families are seated together with an open area for the activities to take place. On their tables, are one or several (depending on the number of tables) letters spelling STEWARDSHIP. In another area are three large boxes wrapped colorfully — with the top of the box wrapped separately for easy removal. The boxes are labeled: (1) God's Gift: Our Beautiful World and Its Creatures; (2) God's Gift of Each Other; (3) God's Gift of ME! The craft and refreshment tables are covered and off to the side.

Activity Summary:

The Gathering begins with the children using letters on their tables to spell stewardship on a wall to focus attention on this theme. Volunteer adults role-play in very brief skits illustrating examples of stewardship and then engage the children and their parents in dialogue. After two "sets" of role-playing, the children gather around one of the gift boxes and remove various items from the box and talk about how the item represented "good stewardship" or "poor stewardship." For the third area of stewardship — "God's Gift of ME!" — the children look for "faces" taped around the room that have pictures on the back (or items attached by bag/yarn/string) that illustrate "good stewardship of self." The children take these clues back to their parents to discuss, and then they present them to the rest of the families and place them in the open box marked "God's Gift of ME!" At the conclusion of the activities with the gift boxes, the families are invited to make three crafts to remember the message of the three areas of stewardship: A bird feeder or a "bird"; a heart-shaped card holding a variety of tea bags to give to a nursing home/senior citizen home/neighbor/grandparent, etc.; and a paper box craft summarizing the overall message of good stewardship.

Supplies for Skit, Gift Boxes, and labels:

- Large candy bar
- School tray "heaped" with food

Stewardship — Taking Care of All God's Gifts

- Full lunch bag
- Three wrapped boxes with removable tops marked: God's Gift of His Beautiful World and Its Creatures; God's Gift of Each Other; Gods Gift of ME!

    — *Inside the "Beautiful World" box:* A bottle filled with drinking water; a garden tool; a small brush or wisk broom; a "recycle" label; a pop can; a camera; a newspaper; some "trash"; a small bird feeder, bird seed, or dog bone; and a Bible

    — *Inside the "God's Gift of Each Other" box:* Greeting cards — birthday, thank you, get well, etc.; a Catholic Relief Service's Rice Bowl, or an advertisement of another children's charity; a toy; a church envelope; a dish towel; a news magazine; a small plastic shovel; a phone; a foreign language/English dictionary; and a Bible.

    — *To place inside the "God's Gift of ME!" box:* A child's face template with the following magazine pictures (on the reverse side) or the actual items attached by bag, tape, or string: Fruits; vegetables; winter clothing — boot, hat, scarf, etc.; sunscreen lotion; alarm clock; toothpaste/toothbrush; soap; sports item; notebook and pencil; book; school; church; musical instrument; dance slipper; and a Bible.

- Labels explaining the meaning of all the above items for each of the three boxes (see page 72)
- child's faces (see face template page 71)

Examples of boxes and their respective contents.

Left to right: Beautiful World box, God's Gifts to Each Other box, God's Gift of Me! box

Script:

Welcome to our Family Gathering on Stewardship! Stewardship is a word a lot of us adults have difficulty understanding — yet the Church considers our attitudes and our actions of stewardship as a very important part of being a follower of Jesus. It is something not one person can figure out alone — we need each other to have stewardship make sense! On your tables are some letters; please bring them up and we will work together to tape the word stewardship on the wall. Today, we are going to talk about stewardship as taking care of all God's gifts. Let's watch and listen closely to an example of stewardship:

Focus: *God's Gift of our Beautiful World and Its Creatures*

Skit #1:

A volunteer strolls into the meeting area, enjoying eating a candy bar, licks her fingers as she finishes it, tosses the candy wrapper on the ground, and walks off out of the room.

Skit #2:

The Narrator holds up a sign that says "School Lunch Room." Two volunteers come in and sit together at a table. One has a tray of food piled high, and the other has a full lunch bag. The script continues:

Volunteer #1: Hey Susie, you sure have a lot of food there — what did you do, buy two lunches? Are you that hungry?

Volunteer #2: Nah, I just like the pudding cup you get with the full lunch, so to get two puddings, my Mom gives me money to buy two lunches. I don't even like the hamburger, and just toss it away — my Mom doesn't know that, though. She really thinks I'm eating all this stuff! What do you bring for lunch?

Volunteer #1: The usual two sandwiches, one peanut butter and one baloney. I can't eat all of it either — hey — it's time, let's go outside for recess.

(Volunteer #1 smashes her full lunch bag and tosses it in the garbage can, and Volunteer #2 dumps the still full tray into the garbage as they both go off together.)

The volunteers return to the open area, carrying the gift box labeled: "God's Gift of our Beautiful World and Its Creatures."

(Volunteers lead the following dialogue:)

Well, boys and girls, what do you think? *(Picking up the candy wrapper on the floor.)* Do you think God is pleased when people throw things on the ground carelessly? What would our world look like if everyone just tossed garbage and papers as they wanted to? (Children will raise their hands for comments.)

What did you think about our lunchroom conversation? (Children will give their opinions on what the skit meant. The volunteer helps the children grasp the point that it is not good stewardship to purposely waste or destroy what He has given.)

Volunteer #2: Boys and girls, come up around our gift box. Inside it are items that will help us understand how God wants us to take care of His beautiful world. I'll need some volunteers to take things out of the box. (*One by one, the following items are taken out of the box and discussed. Inside the box are: a water bottle; a garden tool or watering can; a wisk broom; a "recycle" label; a pop can; a newspaper; some "trash" — candy, gum wrappers; a camera; a small bird feeder/or dog bone, and a Bible, etc. Each item has a label explaining its message. The children will offer their insights as to what each item means as to good stewardship of God's created world. The volunteer also ask for parents to give their comments.*) Moms and Dads, we have different experiences than the children — what are some examples of good stewardship of God's earth that you can share?

Focus: *God's Gift of Each Other*

Narrator: Very good boys and girls, now we are going to look at stewardship as taking care of all God's people — taking care of each other. Let's listen…

Volunteer #1 and #2 walk into the room, pointing and laughing.

Skit:

Volunteer #1: Do you see that new girl — and the outfit she's wearing! How weird! No wonder she's always alone — no one wants to be a friend to someone who looks so different!

Volunteer #2: Hey, is your class collecting money for the people who lost everything in hurricane Katrina?

Volunteer #1: Yeh, but the money my family sends in every week, I'm saving to buy a new CD. My parents won't know — those poor people can just take care of themselves. Why should I give them any help!

Volunteer #2: That's what I think — why should we send money to strangers anyway?

(Volunteers #1 and #2 walk out of the room, and return carrying the gift box labeled: "Taking Care of God's People — Each Other." They lead the following dialogue :)

Well boys and girls, what did you think about the skit? How is it a good or bad example of stewardship — taking care of each other and all God's people? (*Children respond.*) Are there times when we make fun of someone who looks different than we do? How would God want us to behave? We have a box here — let's see what items are inside and figure out together what they mean. (*Inside the box are: Birthday or get well card or thank you note; a Catholic Relief Service's Rice Bowl or picture/small poster of a charity for children; a toy; a church envelope; a dish towel; a news magazine; a small plastic shovel; a phone; a Spanish — or any other language — Dictionary; and a Bible. Each item has a label as to its meaning. The children, their parents, and the volunteers discuss the items as they are taken out of the box one by one. The volunteer also addresses the parents to get their "adult perspective" on taking care of God's people.*)

Focus: "God's Gift of ME!"

Narrator: That's great! We have talked about two types of stewardship — taking care of God's World and taking care of God's People — each other. What is the last type of stewardship we are going to talk about? Yes — taking care of ourselves! Who created us? God did — as the Bible tells us — "Every hair on our heads is counted …" God created us and loves us more than we can ever imagine! Now — sometimes we need to look for clues in our lives to understand what God wants us to do. I see some faces taped around the room — I wonder if they can give us some clues about how God wants us to take care of ourselves. We need volunteers (one from each table if there are too many children to each receive one) to take the faces and the items on them, and go back to your tables and talk about them with your parents. Then we'll ask you to come up and explain the clue to everyone else — and put the face and the items inside this box marked "God's Gift of ME!"

(The faces taped around the room have these magazine/template pictures on the reverse side or the actual item attached in a lunch bag with tape/string: Fruit; vegetable; snow hat/boot or muffler; sunscreen lotion; church; school; book; alarm clock; toothpaste/toothbrush; soap; sports item — football, etc; notebook and pencil; picture of musical instrument or ballet slipper; Bible, etc. Each item is labeled as to its meaning. The Narrator leads the discussion of each item as it is taken out of the box — making sure the parents as well as the children respond and are involved.)

Narrator: We have learned a lot about how to be a good steward of God's gifts! We invite you to go to the craft tables and make three items to take home. These crafts will help us to remember what we talked about today.

Stewardship Crafts:

Bird Feeder Craft

Bird feeder supplies
- Large pinecones
- Yarn
- Bird seed
- Peanut butter
- Margarine and plastic knives
- Plastic bags to take "bird feeder" home

Bird feeder directions
Lay out newspapers to make cleanuup easier.
Tie yarn around the pinecone to hang it later.
"Butter" the pinecones heavily with margarine/peanut butter mixture.
Roll in bird seed.
Place in plastic bag to take home.

Stewardship — Taking Care of All God's Gifts

Bird Craft

Bird craft supplies
- Small (2" or 3") cylinders covered with red construction paper
- Red feathers
- Yellow construction paper beak
- Two goggly eyes
- Glue with glue applicators

Bird craft directions
Cover and glue the cylinders with previously cut-to-size red construction paper.

Glue on feathers, beak, and googly eyes.

Heart Tea Bag Gift

Heart Tea Bag Gift craft supplies
- Construction paper hearts of two sizes
- Glue
- Tea bags
- Cardstock labeled "Share a Cup of Friendship"

Heart Tea Bag Gift directions
Glue the smaller heart at the base of the large heart, leaving the top open to place the tea bags.

Place tea bags.

Glue large heart on card stock labeled "Share a Cup of Friendship."

Fold Up Stewardship Box

Stewardship Box supplies and directions
- Stewardship template
- Fold as indicated on template.

Refreshments:
A variety of *healthy* finger foods: popcorn, carrots, grapes, etc.

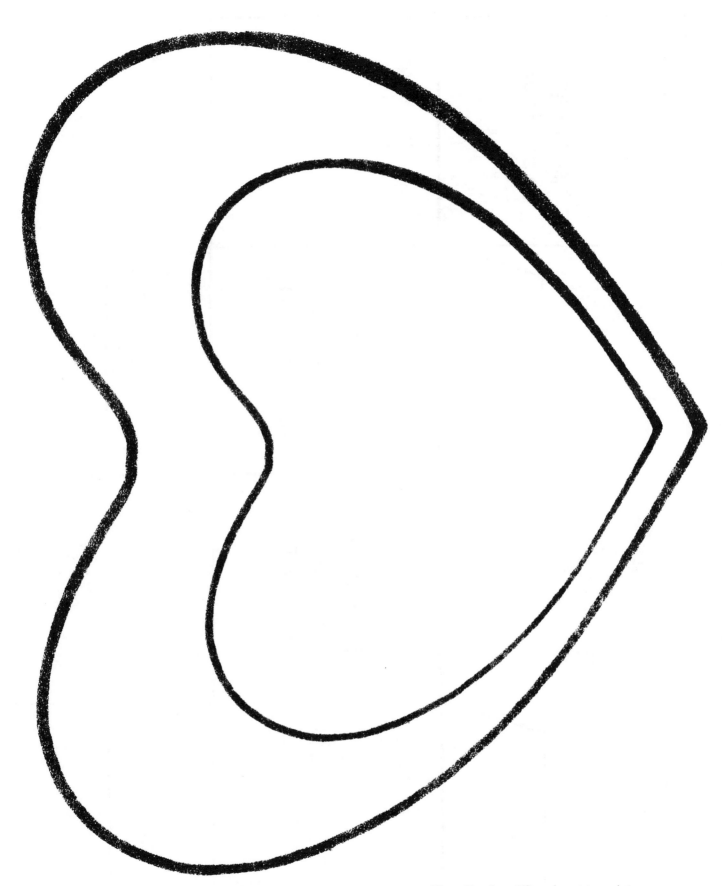

Heart Tea Bag Gift — heart templates

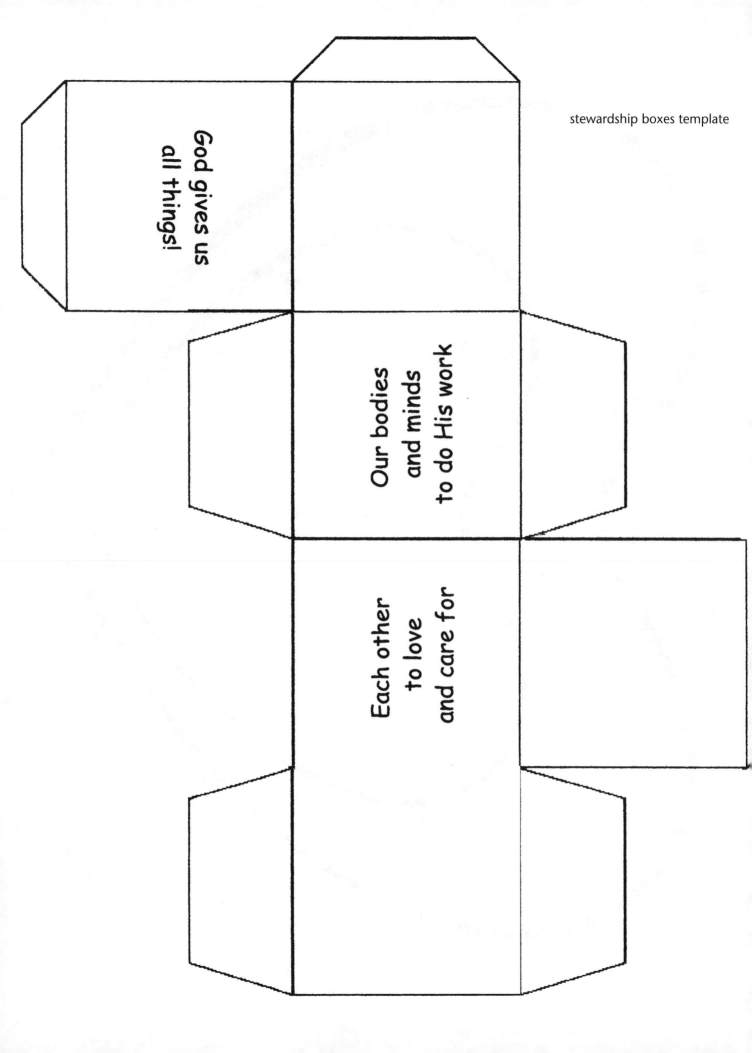

stewardship boxes template

God gives us
all things!

Our bodies
and minds
to do His work

Each other
to love
and care for

Child's face template

Stewardship — Taking Care of All God's Gifts

God's wonderful gifts of clean water to drink and lakes and oceans to swim in need to be protected from pollution!

Look at these cards — a birthday card, get well card, and a thank you card! Sending cards help others not to feel lonely — it tells them we love them.

God asks us to care of ourselves by eating plenty of the healthy fruits and vegetables He created!

Flowers and vegetable gardens help us see how God grows beautiful and delicious things!

In America we are blessed with food to eat every day, warm houses to live in, schools, and churches. When we donate money to good causes we are helping children who don't have what we do.

When we "dress for the weather" — we take good care of our bodies!

God's world needs cleaning up of litter and garbage!

When we share something we love with others, that pleases God!

It helps to protect our skin from too much sun!

Who recycles? What does it do to help our world? When we "re-use" things, it saves our natural resources!

What's this? Who would like to help me explain how this helps us take care of God's people? (When we give to the Church, we know it spreads the message of God's love to everyone who visits or comes to Mass or goes to the school or religion classes.)

Taking time to go to Church and to pray helps us know we are loved by God our Father!

A pop/soda can — a great example of recycling! Who can explain a little more about why we "re-use" cans? (Adults)

A dish towel! When we help around the house, we are showing we care about other people.

Going to school and doing homework helps use our minds to do God's work.

Newspapers — they help us take care of God's world in two ways! We recycle, or re-use, the paper; and when we read newspapers, we know what's happening to others!

Sometimes it is easy to only think about the people around us. News magazines help us know other people need our prayers. God wants us to pray for each other.

Reading books helps us know about the world God created.

What should we do with these wrappers? Pick them up? Leave them on the ground? Throw them away?

Do we sometimes help our parents shovel the snow — or help our neighbors shovel?

Getting enough sleep is important for healthy bodies! How we use the time God gives us is very special too.

A camera helps us remember how beautiful the world is! What is the most beautiful place you have visited?

Taking the time to call someone — someone who might be lonely — is doing God's work. Remember — He expects us to take care of each other.

What do these things have to do with taking care of God's gift of ourselves? (It says in the Bible — Cleanliness is next to Godliness!)

All our animal and bird friends need our care and gentleness too. Remember God made them all — just like He made each of us!

Do you know what this is? It's a dictionary in another language. What does this tell us about taking care of each other? (God wants us to respect EVERYONE — even if we are different from each other.)

Who likes to take a bath? Who takes a bath every day? Does this please God when we take the time to be clean?

On the first page of the Bible, it says God made the earth and all that is in it. He said all creation is "VERY GOOD!"

Remember God's Great Commandment? Love God with all your heart, and love your neighbor as yourself. Who is our neighbor?

Taking care of ourselves means using our muscles for play and sports.

Writing down our special thoughts is one way God speaks to us.

God has given each of us a special talent — maybe it is dancing or playing an instrument or being very good at reading — what do you think your special talent is?

Think of the Great Commandment again: You should love your neighbor AS YOU LOVE YOURSELF! God wants us to take care of ourselves in all these ways.

[labels for God's Gifts boxes]

72

7. MARY, THE FIRST DISCIPLE OF JESUS

Objective:

To recognize Mary, the Mother of Jesus, as the first disciple of Jesus; as a loving Mother available to all of us in our daily life; and as an example of trust and obedience to God's will.

Activity Summary:

The families are seated in an arrangement enabling all to see and participate in an echo pantomime about the life of Mary. The children are asked to stand together to see and mimic the motions of the mime acting out the words of the Narrator. Following this, parents and children are invited to trace the child's body with the heading, "I am part of Jesus' family too!" Three additional crafts are available: The rosary card with Scripture passages; the "Mary" tea light candle; and the Mother and Child lace-up picture.

Activity Setting:

Tables and chairs, with an open space for the children to be involved with the echo pantomime. Craft and refreshment tables are off to the side.

Script:

Welcome to our Family Gathering on Mary, the Mother of Jesus. Who would like to share some stories you know about Mary that you have heard in Church or in your religion classes?

(After the children share): You already know a lot about her and the special place she holds in our faith. To help us remember her relationship with Jesus and with us, we invite you to follow along with the actions of the mime as we listen to this story of Mary.

Echo Pantomime: Mary, the First Disciple of Jesus

Today we remember Mary,

   (mime holds up calendar, pointing to the date and her head while nodding)

the Mother of Jesus and His first disciple.

   (rock a baby in her arms and puts one finger up)

Mary was a young girl about fifteen years old,

   (holds up ten fingers, then five more)

when an angel of God named Gabriel,

   (flap angel wings)

visited her in her home.

Mary, The First Disciple of Jesus

Mary was so surprised and afraid!

(look surprised and then place hands over face)

Loud voice from an unseen source: "DO NOT BE AFRAID, MARY. YOU HAVE FOUND FAVOR WITH GOD! YOU WILL HAVE A SON — YOU ARE TO NAME HIM JESUS, THE SON OF THE MOST HIGH!"

(looks up and removes her hands from covering her face)

Mary said, "I am the handmaiden of the Lord, let it be done according to His will."

(smiles, looks upward, and nods)

Now, when it became time for the baby Jesus to be born,

(hold hands out as to show a large stomach)

Mary and her husband, Joseph,

(hook arm around someone imaginary)

were on a journey to Bethlehem to be counted in a census.

(count fingers)

Mary was very tired and she was riding on a donkey.

(put hand to head as if very tired, and move up and down as if riding on a donkey)

Jesus was born in a stable, and placed in a manger.

(rock baby and place him in a manger)

Mary and Joseph were good parents and taught Jesus many things about our loving Father in Heaven.

(hands teaching and holding them up to Heaven)

When Jesus was a grown man,

(reach up high as if patting him on the back)

Mary, Jesus, and His friends went to a wedding.

(dance around festively)

The wine had run out, and the guests needed more.

(hold an imaginary jug upside down and shake it)

Mary told the friends of Jesus to bring Him jugs of water.

(carry imaginary jugs and put them down)

Jesus changed the water to wine!

(look surprised, with hand to mouth in amazement)

This was the first miracle of Jesus.

(hold up one finger)

Mary loved Jesus so much!

(hug with arms crossed on chest)

She always believed in Him and never left Him.

(arms still crossed on chest, now nods head in agreement)

When Jesus died on the cross, Mary was there.

(put head down very sadly)

She was there at the tomb on Easter morning after the resurrection!

(joyous, arms flung wide)

Mary is our Mother too — she loves us and takes our prayers to Jesus.

(blows kisses to all and looks up to Heaven)

(Motions now stop and Narrator continues talking about the rosary.)

Catholics have special prayer beads, called a rosary, that help us remember the events in the lives of Jesus and Mary. We will make one today for you to take home to remind us that Mary was the first disciple of Jesus, and that she is our Mother too. We are all part of the family of Jesus! We invite the parents to trace their child and write on the figure — "We are part of Jesus' family." The next craft we invite you to make is a "Mary" tea light candle. Mary let the light of Jesus shine through her life! Glue small pieces of colored tissue paper on the baby food jar and sprinkle it with glitter. When you light the candle inside, the light will come through. This helps us remember that we each need to be like Mary, allowing Jesus to shine through us. And we have a beautiful picture of Mary with her baby, Jesus, for you to lace up and place in a very special place in your home.

Mary Crafts Supplies and Directions:

Rosary Craft

Supplies
- Copies of rosary picture on cardstock (template provided on page 77).
- Small pom poms or flowers.
- Glue and glue applicators.

Directions
Glue a flower or pom pom onto a rose bead for every prayer said.

Body Tracing Craft

Supplies
- Large (3 feet wide, or more) paper and crayons or markers

Instructions
Parents trace their child's outline onto the paper and write, " _____ is part of Jesus' Family too!"

Child draws in the features and details.

Mary, The First Disciple of Jesus

"Mary" Tea Lights

Supplies
- Baby food jars
- Tissue papers in a variety of colors
- Scissors
- White glue and water
- Glitter (if desired)
- Small votive candle

Directions
Mix glue and water (50-50).

Tear or cut tissue.

Turn jar upside down.

Spread a thin layer of glue on the bottom and sides.

Attach paper shapes.

Paint a thin coat of glue mixture over all the paper.

Sprinkle glitter.

When dry, add candle inside.

Mary Picture Lace-Up

Supplies
- Copy of Madonna and Child template (see page 78) on 8.5" x 11" cardstock with holes
- punched at 2-inch intervals along border
- 6' length of narrow ribbon or yarn

Directions
Thread ribbon or yarn in and out through holes, tie at bottom.

Refreshments:

Tea, coffee, and lemonade. Cookies, scones, or cupcakes. Decorations are nice in blue and white or flowered cloths.

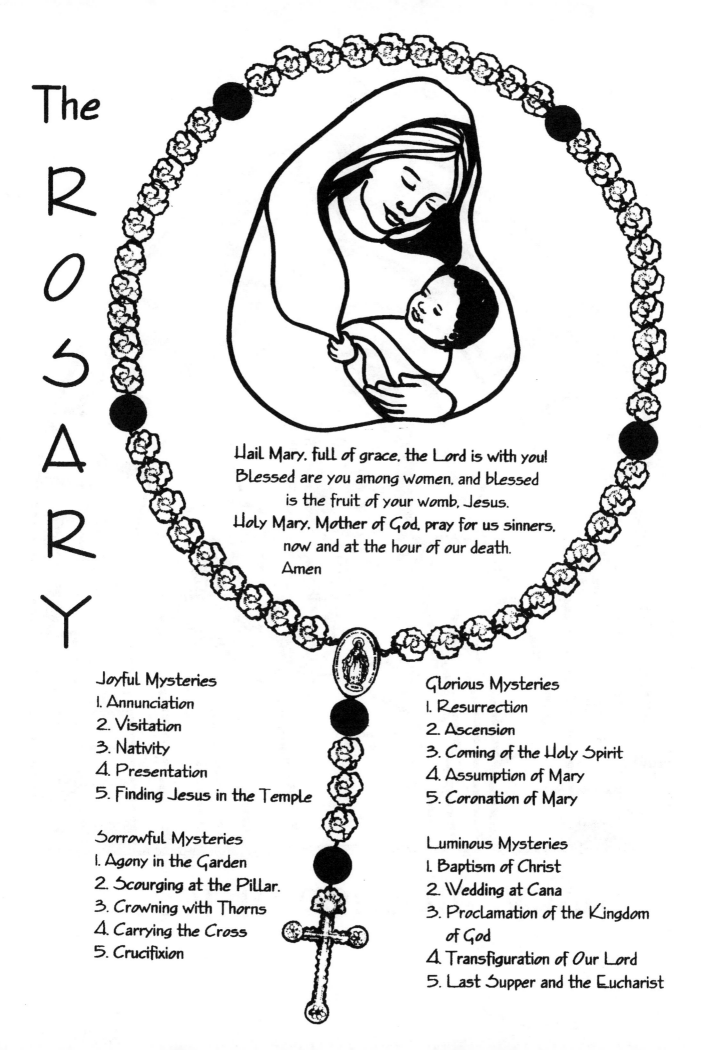

The

ROSARY

Hail Mary, full of grace, the Lord is with you!
Blessed are you among women, and blessed
is the fruit of your womb, Jesus.
Holy Mary, Mother of God, pray for us sinners,
now and at the hour of our death.
Amen

Joyful Mysteries
1. Annunciation
2. Visitation
3. Nativity
4. Presentation
5. Finding Jesus in the Temple

Sorrowful Mysteries
1. Agony in the Garden
2. Scourging at the Pillar.
3. Crowning with Thorns
4. Carrying the Cross
5. Crucifixion

Glorious Mysteries
1. Resurrection
2. Ascension
3. Coming of the Holy Spirit
4. Assumption of Mary
5. Coronation of Mary

Luminous Mysteries
1. Baptism of Christ
2. Wedding at Cana
3. Proclamation of the Kingdom
   of God
4. Transfiguration of Our Lord
5. Last Supper and the Eucharist

MARY, MOTHER OF JESUS

8. THE PARABLES OF JESUS

Objective:

To explore the parables of The Sower and the Seeds, the Prodigal Son, the Lost Sheep, and the Good Samaritan through engaging the children in skits and take-home crafts.

Activity Summary:

The children and their parents are welcomed and the children given their "parts" through neck signs. All are asked to sit facing an empty area with the scene of rocks (boxes covered in brown paper — with scrunched newspaper on the top and sides of the boxes to give more of a rocky unevenness before covering them with the brown paper), stream (blue tablecloth), and bushes (plants). The children are involved in various roles as well as the "Chorus" for the four parable skits. After each skit, we explain briefly the meaning of the parable in our lives today, as well as show the children the corresponding craft they will make to remember the parable.

Activity Setting:

Skit area as described above, and tables covered for glue protection with craft items. Refreshment table as desired.

Activity Supplies:

Supplies needed for each activity are listed immediately before each script.

Script:

Welcome everyone to our Family Gathering on four parables of Jesus. We know that Jesus many times taught His followers through telling them simple stories. Stories like we are going to act out today. Through each of these skits, we will be needing your help! Please keep your eyes and ears open and be ready to do your part. Also, after each skit, we are going to show you an example of a craft that you can make to take home and remember the lesson Jesus taught us. We also have a label to stick on the back of your craft with an important message.

Now let's begin with the "Prodigal Son." Prodigal is a big word that means someone who is very wasteful, and in this case it refers to a son who is very wasteful with his Father's money. We will need your help each time we hold up a large sign that says a word that you are to say together. You have an important part to do, so keep your eyes ready for the signs!

The Parables of Jesus

The Prodigal Son

Props and Characters:

- Son 1
- Son 2
- Narrator
- Chorus (Audience)
- Large Signs Needed (*for the Chorus — the Chorus is the audience of parents and children who yell out the word when the appropriate sign is held up*):

ONE   TWO   BYE!   OOOOOOH! NOOOOOO!   TOUGH LUCK!
NO FOOD! NO HOME!   OINK! OINK!   YUCK!   THANK GOODNESS!
IT'S ABOUT TIME!   LOOK! IT'S HIM!   (CLAP) HURRAY! PARTY!
WHO?   YEAH! HOW COME DAD?   (NOD — GOD LOVES US!)

- Labels to place on the back of the craft, "God always welcomes us home to His Love and Forgiveness."

Script:

Narrator: There was a man who had two sons.

Chorus says "ONE" — when first son comes up and bows; Chorus says "TWO" — when the second son comes up and bows.

Son 1:   "Hey Dad, could I have half of all that you own — it will belong to me one day!"

Narrator: So the Father divided the property and gave half to his son. A few days later, the younger son took all his money and went off to parts unknown. (Son 1 holds up a sign with a ? and walks out of the room on a "path" — strip of brown or white paper — where the words "Parts Unknown" are written. His clothing is "fairly fancy.")

Chorus: (Yells) BYE!!

Narrator: But he wasted all his money on foolish things!

Chorus: OOOOOOOOH NOOOOOOOO!

Narrator: He spent all of it! He was homeless and hungry!

(Son 1 returns with ragged clothes, holding a sign that says — NO FOOD! NO HOME!)

Chorus: TOUGH LUCK!

Narrator: He was so hungry he took a job feeding pigs.

(Son 1 pretends to throw food on the ground for the pigs, then looks hungrily at it — or smells it dreamily before throwing it on the ground.)

Chorus: OINK! OINK!

Narrator: He even wanted to eat the pigs' food!

Chorus: YUCK!

Narrator: Then he remembered how loving his Father was —- and how he always had a warm place to stay and food to eat.

Chorus: THANK GOODNESS!

Narrator: The son said —

Son 1: I think I'll go home and say, "I'm sorry, Dad, please forgive me."

Chorus: IT'S ABOUT TIME!

Narrator: While he was still a long way off, his Father saw him.

Chorus: LOOK! IT'S HIM!

Son 1: Dad, I'm sorry, please forgive me. (Son 1 hangs his head down in shame.)

Chorus: (CLAPS — and says Hurray!)

Narrator: And they started to have a party!

Chorus: (Puts on party hats — or hold up signs that say "PARTY.")

Narrator: Remember the older brother?

Chorus: WHO?

Narrator: Well, he was really angry. He had stayed at home and worked very hard all the time his younger brother was out wasting his Father's money! And now — his Father was having a huge party for his brother, and he wasn't even invited!

Son 2: Listen Dad! How come you give this creep a party who wasted all your money!

Chorus: YEAH! HOW COME DAD?

Narrator: And the Father said,

Father: Everything I have now belongs to you, but we should be happy because your brother, who was lost, is found!

Chorus: CLAPS and yells HURRAY!

Narrator: Now, boys and girls, if this is the way an ordinary Dad treats his son…

Chorus: Yeah?

Narrator: How much better will our God in Heaven treat us?

Chorus: (Sign says NOD!)

Narrator: Sometimes we all do things that are like "wandering" down the wrong path. Things that take us away from our loving relationship with God. Things that we have said or done that we wish we hadn't done.

From this parable that Jesus told, we know that God our Father is always waiting and watching for us to come back to Him. He never stops loving us and wants to welcome us home to Him. To help you remember this story, we have a "Welcome Home" door knob hanger for you to decorate and take home. (*Craft directions and supplies are listed at the end of the four parable scripts.*)

Now let's listen to our next parable about a farmer.

The Sower of the Seeds

Props and Characters:
- Narrator
- Farmer — straw hat, scarf, etc., perhaps overalls, and carrying a basket of "seeds"
- The Sun (teen or youth helper) — see costume suggestion art below
- Basket of seeds — cut construction paper with a seed taped on it
- Teens or older children who are hidden behind the rocks, with the droopy and strong flowers, and the thorny branches

- A footpath — (Use the same "Parts Unknown" path; simply remove that sign and put a sign saying "Footpath" on it.)
- Neck signs that say BIRDS!
- Rocky ground — boxes wrapped as "rocks" — with sign that says ROCKY GROUND
- THORNY GROUND — boxes covered with branches, sticks, etc.
- Droopy flowers (thin tissue paper blossoms that droop) on sticks
- Strong flowers (plastic or made from construction paper or foam board) on sticks
- Green tablecloth with plants to represent GOOD SOIL — with a sign also
- Dress for the "Sun" — plastic construction hard hat with slits through it and "flames" protruding and yellow table cloth poncho
- If desired, "neck signs" that say "Good Soil!" with a sunflower seed taped on it (paper with holes punched and string attached to place around the children's necks)
(The reverse side of these signs could have a picture of a "sheep" to be used in the "Lost Sheep" parable. See page 96 for sheep face template.)

Sun hat — costume suggestion for Sun character. See instructions for creating this hat on page 96.

(As described in the Activity Summary, the setting of rocks, water, etc. has been prepared. The Narrator places "Rocky Ground," "Thorny Ground," and "Good Soil" at various spots in the scene and replaces the "Parts Unknown" with "Footpath." The teen helpers are hidden behind the "rocks.")

A few children have been given the "neck signs" that say "BIRDS!"

Labels for craft say, "We are good soil for faith to grow!"

Script:

Narrator: One day a farmer went out sowing his seeds.

(Farmer comes out with his basket of seeds.)

Part of what he sowed landed on a footpath, where birds came along and ate them up.

(Farmer throws seeds on the "Footpath" and the children with the "BIRD" signs come up and scoop the seeds up.)

Narrator: Part of it fell on rocky ground, where it had little soil. It sprouted at once.

(Farmer throws seeds on the rocky ground and the helpers behind the rocks sprout up the strong flowers.)

But as the soil had no depth, when the sun rose, *(the "Sun" comes out and stands before the flowers)* and scorched it, the flower began to wither for lack of roots. *(Helper behind the rocks, puts up the droopy flowers when the "Sun" comes out.)* Part of the seed fell among thorns, which grew up *(Helpers pop up strong flowers, and another hidden helper with thorns knocks down the flowers)* and choked it. Part of it finally landed on good soil where it yielded grain a hundred fold! *(Helpers hold up all the strong flowers.)*

Narrator: Good soil is like us! God gives us the seeds of faith to grow. What will help us grow is praying, learning about God, and going to Church. When we do these things, we will grow very beautifully like the flowers we are going to make today to remember the message of this parable.

To help all of us remember that we are "good soil" that will grow strong flowers of faith, we have cut out sunflowers and stems. You can make green tissue paper leaves and stems, and glue on bird or sunflower seeds in the middle.

The Good Samaritan

Props and Characters:
(We use only four actors, who quickly change and play multiple roles.)
- Narrator
- Injured Man
- Robbers
- Priest
- Levite
- Good Samaritan
- Innkeeper
- Chorus of audience that will "stomp" their feet whenever the sign "FOOTSTEPS" is held up, and also will "MOAN" when the sign is shown.
- Costumes for Priest, Levite, Good Samaritan, Innkeeper, Robbers, Injured Man (They can be very simple — black armbands for the robbers, etc.)
- Large signs for the Chorus:
  - FOOTSTEPS   MOAN   LISTEN
  - OUCH! (several large and in red to put on the Injured Man)
  - PAIN! SAD! (To be held up by the Injured Man when the script is read)
- Bandages
- Gold coins
- Sign for path (used previously as "Footpath" and "Parts Unknown": Different Road
- Sign that reads "Inn"
- Labels to place on the completed craft, "Love one another."

Script:

One day a man thought he could ask Jesus a question that couldn't be answered: "Who is my neighbor?"

Jesus answered him by telling this story:

One day, a man traveling all alone was suddenly attacked by a group of thieves who robbed him, beat him, and left him half dead by the side of the road.

The Parables of Jesus

(Robbers quickly run over and stick signs that say "Ouch!" on the traveler, who falls to the ground.)

As he lay there in pain and misery *(the injured man holds up signs that say "Pain!" "Misery!"),* he heard footsteps. (Chorus stomps feet as "FOOTSTEPS" sign is held up.)

"Ah! I hear someone coming! I hope he will help me!" thought the injured man. He waited and listened (Chorus cups their ear as if intently listening when the LISTEN sign is held up) for what seemed like hours, as the footsteps (FOOTSTEPS sign) faded away.

It had happened that a Priest had been walking down the road, but when he saw the injured man, he decided to take a different road. He was in a hurry and didn't want to be bothered with this today! *(Priest starts to walk by, then peering into the distance, quickly takes the "Different Road.")*

After a little while, the injured man heard footsteps again! (FOOTSTEPS sign) He wanted to call out to get someone to help him, but all he could do was moan (MOAN sign is held up). This time, surely someone would stop! The man was a Levite, a well-known teacher in the temple. When the Levite saw the man lying on the side of the road, he turned his head and quickly walked by!

It wasn't too long until the man heard another set of footsteps! (FOOTSTEPS sign) He wanted to believe that this person would reach down and help him. He was losing hope and was sure he was going to die right there on the side of the road.

The man who was traveling down the road this time was a stranger from Samaria. No one even liked people from Samaria! They were different from ordinary people, and avoided at all costs! But as the Samaritan passed down the road, he noticed the beaten man and feeling sorry for him, he bent down to get a closer look at the wounds. Gently, he wrapped bandages on the sores and carefully helped the injured man to walk to the nearest inn. *(The Good Samaritan removes the "Ouch!" signs and replaces them with bandages. He lifts the injured man up and helps him to walk to the Innkeeper. The Innkeeper greets them and has a seat prepared for the injured man to rest.)* He stayed with the man overnight and took care of him.

The next morning he had to leave, but he knew the injured man needed more rest and healing. He gave the Innkeeper money and said, "Take care of him, feed him, and make sure he has everything he needs. If I owe more money, I will pay the bill the next time I am here."

Jesus said to the man who had asked the question, "Now, which one of these three men was a neighbor to the injured man?" The man answered, "The one who stopped and helped him."

Jesus said, "You go and do the same."

Boys and girls, would anyone like to tell us the meaning of this parable? (Invite the children to come up and answer the question.)

To help us remember that everyone is our neighbor, we have pictures of windows and shapes to draw faces, where you can draw in your neighbor, or your imagined neighbor. We also have a sticker of Jesus to place in a window too.

The label we have for you to put on your house to remind you of this parable says, "Love One Another."

Now, we have our last parable for today, the story of "The Lost Sheep."

The Lost Sheep

Props and Characters:
- Jesus as the Good Shepherd — staff and brown robe
- Lost Sheep
- Herd of Sheep (The children have reversed their "Good Soil" neck signs to show the sheep picture on the other side, and are now sitting around the rocks and stream.)
- Same setting as before with rocks and stream and grassy area
- Label to place on the back of the craft: Jesus is like the Good Shepherd, He loves each of us in a special way!

Script:
Narrator: Boys and girls, we would like to tell you the story of the Good Shepherd.

A long time ago, there was a shepherd who had 100 sheep. He was very proud of his sheep and loved each one in a very special way. Every day he took the sheep to eat sweet grass and to drink cool water. He kept them safe from wild animals.

(Shepherd walks in and walks around the room, patting different sheep, and saying things like "Your wool looks so white today;" "How is the grass — sweet enough?"; and so on.)

Narrator: One night, the shepherd counted his sheep.

(Shepherd starts pointing and counting with exaggeration.)

(One previously selected student, already sitting at the side of the group, wanders away, looking curious as to what is happening elsewhere beyond the confines of the meadow they are in now. He peeks in the "bushes," crosses the "stream," slowly meandering around the room.)
(Shepherd looking very worried, again starts pointing and counting his sheep.)

Narrator: One lamb was lost! The shepherd left the other sheep in a safe place. Then he looked everywhere for the lost sheep! He climbed rocks and pushed through thorny bushes, he crossed streams, and he called and called!

(The shepherd may wish to huddle the sheep together and pat them on the head, before he begins his search for the lost one. He then gazes around the room, scratches his head, looks in the bushes, crosses the streams, peeks around the rocks, etc.)

The Parables of Jesus

Narrator: It was getting dark, and the shepherd was afraid of a wild animal finding the lost sheep before he did!

(The lost sheep looks up in the sky, begins to act afraid, and curls up with his knees to his chest, looking scared as the night approaches.)

Narrator: At last the shepherd found the lost lamb! He was so happy that his little sheep was safe! He hugged the sheep and brought it back to the others.

Shepherd: Thank goodness I've found you! You are safe now. The other sheep will be happy to have you home with us! Look! I've found him!

Shepherd (addressing the children): Boys and girls, the Good Shepherd is like Jesus. He wants us to know from this story that no matter where we wander away, He will always look for us until He finds us because He loves us so much!

Narrator: To remind you of this story, we have sheep faces for you to decorate and take home today. The sticker on the back of this craft will say: "Jesus is like the Good Shepherd, He loves each of us in a special way!"

Parables Crafts:

Welcome Home Door Knob Hanger

Supplies
- Foam door knob hanger (available at craft stores)
- Colored paper and foam shapes
- Markers, glue, scissors
- Tiny bells, narrow ribbon
- "Welcome" (templates provided — see page 88) copied on colored paper
- Label: God always welcomes us home to His Love and Forgiveness (see page 89)

Directions
Decorate door hanger.
Punch small hole on bottom edge.
Thread ribbon into the hole and tie on little bell.
Place label on back.

Good Soil Flowers

Supplies
- Sunflower shapes cut from yellow cardstock (template on page 90)
- Green cardboard stems, green tissue paper
- Glue, and glue applicators
- Birdseed
- Label: We Are Good Soil for Faith to Grow! (see page 91)

Directions

Glue flower and stem together (can add crumpled tissue paper to stem if desired).

Apply glue and birdseed to flower.

Place label on back.

Good Neighbor Craft

Supplies

- Window template (see page 92) copied onto colored paper or cardstock
- Crayons and markers
- Glue and glue applicators
- Jesus stickers
- Label: Love One Another (see page 93)

Directions

Draw or cut out faces of neighbors to glue into windows.

Place Jesus sticker in one of the windows.

Place label on back.

Sheep Faces

Supplies

- Paper plates
- Sheep ears and mouth template (see page 94)
- Cotton balls, googly eyes, pink pom-poms (for noses)
- Glue and glue applicators
- Ribbon
- Labels: Jesus is like the Good Shepherd, He loves each of us in a special way! (See page 95)

Directions

Glue cotton to cover the paper plate.

Glue on eyes, nose, and ribbon.

Place label on back.

Refreshments:

Cookies, beverages

WELCOME

WELCOME

WELCOME

WELCOME

WELCOME

God always welcomes us home to His Love and Forgiveness.

God always welcomes us home to His Love and Forgiveness.

God always welcomes us home to His Love and Forgiveness.

God always welcomes us home to His Love and Forgiveness.

God always welcomes us home to His Love and Forgiveness.

God always welcomes us home to His Love and Forgiveness.

God always welcomes us home to His Love and Forgiveness.

God always welcomes us home to His Love and Forgiveness.

God always welcomes us home to His Love and Forgiveness.

God always welcomes us home to His Love and Forgiveness.

God always welcomes us home to His Love and Forgiveness.

God always welcomes us home to His Love and Forgiveness.

God always welcomes us home to His Love and Forgiveness.

God always welcomes us home to His Love and Forgiveness.

We Are Good Soil for
Faith to Grow!

We Are Good Soil for
Faith to Grow

We Are Good Soil for
Faith to Grow

We Are Good Soil for
Faith to Grow

We Are Good Soil for
Faith to Grow

We Are Good Soil for
Faith to Grow

We Are Good Soil for
Faith to Grow

We Are Good Soil for
Faith to Grow

We Are Good Soil for
Faith to Grow

We Are Good Soil for
Faith to Grow

We Are Good Soil for
Faith to Grow

We Are Good Soil for
Faith to Grow

We Are Good Soil for
Faith to Grow

We Are Good Soil for
Faith to Grow

Where is my neighbor?

Love One Another

Love One Another

Love One Another

Love One Another

Love One Another

Love One Another

Love One Another

Love One Another

Love One Another

Love One Another

Love One Another

Love One Another

Love One Another

Love One Another

[Sheep ears and mouth templates for Sheep Faces craft on page 87.]

Jesus is like the Good Shepherd,
He loves each of us
in a special way!

Jesus is like the Good Shepherd,
He loves each of us
in a special way!

Jesus is like the Good Shepherd,
He loves each of us
in a special way!

Jesus is like the Good Shepherd,
He loves each of us
in a special way!

Jesus is like the Good Shepherd,
He loves each of us
in a special way!

Jesus is like the Good Shepherd,
He loves each of us
in a special way!

Jesus is like the Good Shepherd,
He loves each of us
in a special way!

Jesus is like the Good Shepherd,
He loves each of us
in a special way!

Jesus is like the Good Shepherd,
He loves each of us
in a special way!

Jesus is like the Good Shepherd,
He loves each of us
in a special way!

Jesus is like the Good Shepherd,
He loves each of us
in a special way!

Jesus is like the Good Shepherd,
He loves each of us
in a special way!

Jesus is like the Good Shepherd,
He loves each of us
in a special way!

Jesus is like the Good Shepherd,
He loves each of us
in a special way!

[Sheep face template for signs for Parable of Lost Sheep activity]

Sun Hat instructions

- Carefully cut holes into a yellow hat with a utility knife. (Use a construction worker's "hardhat" from a toy department, a salad bowl, or half of a yellow ball.)
- Cut long triangular "rays" from yellow craft foam or stiff paper, wider at the base than the holes in the hat.
- Slightly roll one end of each ray to fit into the holes.

9. THE MIRACLES OF JESUS

Objective:

To provide families the opportunity to interact with each other as they create an impromptu play based on one of four miracles.

Activity Summary:

As each family arrives for the Gathering, they are given a slip of paper with one of these miracles listed: "The Loaves and the Fishes"; "The Wedding at Cana"; "Walking on Water"; and "Raising of Lazarus." Families group together to prepare a play for the other families, using props, simple costumes, and a designated Scripture passage. The costume or prop representing Jesus will be the same for each play (to help children recognize Him). After the performances, the families are invited to make a craft to remember the miracle and to enjoy a time of hospitality.

Activity Setting:

The room has four areas at some distance from each other with props, costumes and Scripture passages. Each of the four areas has a sign with one miracle listed. There is a large empty center area for acting out the plays. Craft and refreshment tables are off to the side.

Props and Costumes Needed:

Loaves and Fishes

- Basket with loaves and fishes (designed with a false bottom)
- Pieces of muslin or squares of cloth with rope ties for head coverings
- Green grass and hill setting (green and brown plastic table cloths with plants or covered boxes)
- Additional baskets
- Simple tunic costumes, head coverings (child size)
- Large name tags (8.5" X 11" paper with name clearly printed, hole punched on sides with yarn attached to wear around neck) used to identify main characters
- Special item to identify Jesus like a tunic in a distinctive color or a halo, beard, etc.
- Scripture: Mark 6:34-44

Walking on Water

- A "boat" made from folding chairs arranged in a row, possibly covered with dark paper
- A fan as the wind "coming up" — or could have some of the group "blow" loudly

The Miracles of Jesus

- Simple costumes and head coverings
- Blue table cloths to represent the water
- Scripture: Matthew 14:22-33

Raising of Lazarus

- A tomb — large cardboard box
- Rolls of white toilet paper to wrap Lazarus, cloth for his face
- A stone (could be children wearing "stone" signs as they crouch before the tomb)
- Simple costumes, head coverings, and the special item to represent Jesus
- Scripture: John 11:38-44

Wedding at Cana

- Festive setting, balloons, fancier costumes for the bride and groom
- Large jugs (milk jugs decorated)
- Chief Servant with chef's hat, etc.
- Other simple costumes and head coverings, plus the Jesus identifying piece
- Scripture: John 2:1 - 11

Script:

Welcome to our Family Gathering on the miracles of Jesus! We know that Jesus performed many miracles, healing people of sicknesses of body, mind, and spirit. He showed love in everything He did. Today, we are going to ask you to act out one of these miracles. When you came in today, each family got a slip of paper naming one of four miracles. We have signs in four areas of the room to identify where you'll go to work on your play together. At each of the areas, there are props, simple costumes, and a Scripture passage. You'll have about 20 minutes to prepare your play. We hope you enjoy working with each other! We won't start the timer on the 20 minutes until each group gathers in their spot and has 5 or 10 minutes to introduce themselves. Please feel free to be as creative as possible!

Craft Supplies and Instructions:

Fish Craft

Supplies

- Fish template (see page 101) — make enough copies to use for craft and the "Loaves and Fishes" skit
- Shiny foil wrapping paper
- Glue and glue applicators

Directions

Cut shiny paper into fin shapes.
Glue onto the fish.

Lazarus Pop-up Card

Supplies
• 3 pages (template provided on pages 102–104) to copy, fold, and glue.

Directions
Fold cover text page in half, printed side out. Set aside.

Fold tomb scene in half, blank side out. This is the card's inside.

With the folded edge of the "inside" on your left, fold down the top corner to make a triangle (a).

Unfold the triangle and open the card. There should be an upside down triangle at the top of the page. Pull the triangle toward you (b).

Press the fold lines in the opposite direction of the original folds so that the triangle points forward (c).

Glue the inside of the card to the cover. *Be careful not to get glue in the triangle area.*

Fold the Lazarus figure down the center and glue the bottom half to the inside triangle (d).

{a} Fold down the top left corner of the folded "inside" card.

{b} Open the card and pull the triangle toward you.

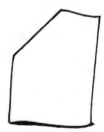

{c} after folding the triangle so that it points forward, the closed card should look like this.

{d} Glue the bottom half of the folded Lazarus figure to the inside triangle.

The Miracles of Jesus

Water to Wine Craft

Supplies

For each wheel:

- One small paper plate
- One top wheel (copy template on page 105 onto card stock)
- One paper fastener
- Two semicircles of colored paper (approximately 4-1/4" in diameter; suggest blue and red)
- Glue.

Directions

Prepare the top circle by cutting an opening into the center of the water jug.

Prepare the base circle (paper plate) by gluing one semicircle of each color to form one circle in the center.

Poke a small hole through the center of both circles and attach the paper fastener so that the top circle rotates freely.

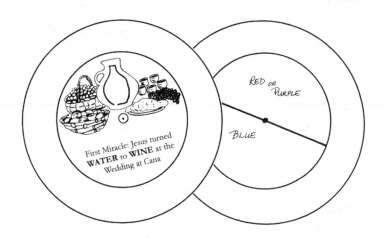

Refreshments:

Blue jello in clear plastic cups with people crackers on top

"I am the resurrection and the life;
whoever believes in me, even if he dies, will live,
and everyone who lives and believes in me will never die."

So Jesus came to the tomb.
It was a cave, and a stone lay across it.
Jesus said, "Take away the stone."
Martha, the dead man's sister, said to him,
"Lord, by now there will be a stench;
he has been dead for four days."
Jesus said to her,
"Did I not tell you that if you believe
you will see the glory of God?"
So they took away the stone.
And He cried out in a loud voice,
"Lazarus, come out!"
The dead man came out,
tied hand and foot with burial bands,
and his face was wrapped in a cloth.

Now many who had come and seen
what he had done, began to believe in him.

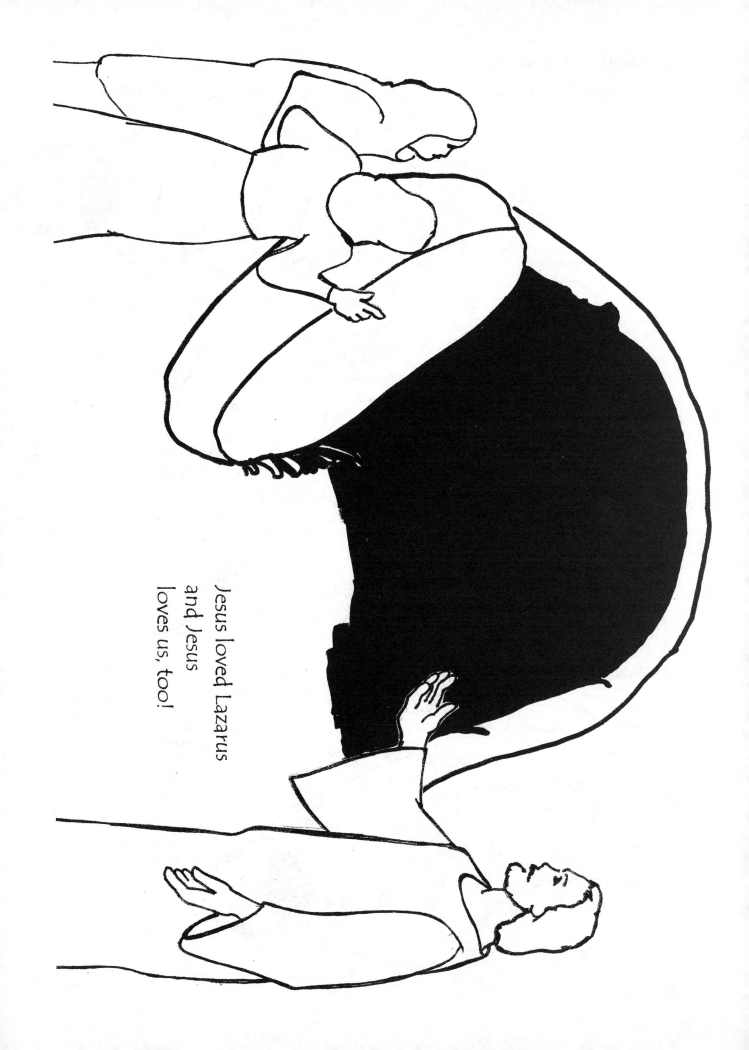

Jesus loved Lazarus
and Jesus
loves us, too!

First Miracle: Jesus turned **WATER** to **WINE** at the Wedding at Cana

First Miracle: Jesus turned **WATER** to **WINE** at the Wedding at Cana

Project Checklist

_____

_____

_____

_____

_____

_____

_____

_____

_____

_____

_____

_____

_____

_____

_____

_____

_____

_____

_____

10. FOOD AND GAMES IN THE TIME OF JESUS

Theme:

To help families connect with the human side of Jesus. As a child He did many of the things we do today.

Activity Summary:

Families enjoy tasting the foods and playing the games that were common at the time of Jesus. Following these activities, they are invited to make the board game of *Mancala* and a set of *Knucklebones* to take home.

Activity Setting:

Tables are set with natural colored woven cloths or placemats. Each table has a basket or ceramic bowl/plate with a sampling of some of the food Jesus would have eaten: almonds, pistachios, parsley, mint, sage, cinnamon, olives, dates, grapes, "locusts" (candy bugs), fava or garbanzo beans, cucumbers, lemons or oranges, garlic, onions, horseradish, honey, turnips, beets, lettuce, dandelion, dried fish, milk, wine, and bread (dark or unleavened). If more convenient, one display table with these above items could be used instead.

The board game of *Mancala* and the game of *Knucklebones* are placed on tables with a volunteer ready to explain how to play.

A separate area is set for the active games of bowling, catch (with soft balls like hackeysacks), hopscotch (chalked or taped onto the floor), slingshots target (with soft "shots" such as air-dried small marshmallows), and scarves or beanbags for juggling. (If available), a sand table with blocks or tubes creating a "maze" for marbles to pass through is prepared also.

The craft tables and refreshment tables are off to the side.

Script:

Welcome to our Family Gathering on the life of Jesus as a child! Do you see foods that you eat at home on your tables? Of the ones you see, what is your favorite one? Are there foods there that you eat every day? What is different from what your family eats?

A lot has changed since Jesus was a little boy in Nazareth, but in many ways He was like any of the children here today. He probably had favorite toys and played games with His friends.

Food and Games in the Time of Jesus

Today, we are going to not only enjoy tasting the foods He ate, but also learn and play with the games and toys popular during His childhood.

How many of you play board games? They were used a lot in the time of Jesus. We have several tables set up for you to try them out.

Running, catch, wrestling, hopscotch, juggling, slingshot targets (remember David and Goliath?), and playing with marbles through mazes were also very popular. Please feel free to walk around and play some of the games. Then, we have two games for you to make and take home: *Mancala* and *Knucklebones!*

Active Games:

Hopscotch — tape or chalk pattern on floor

Catch — hackeysacks

Sand Table — with tubes creating a maze for marbles to pass through

Slingshots — soft targets (air-dried marshmallows)

Juggling — beanbags or scarves

Bowling — soft items to "knock over" with ball

Race — area to compete running speeds

Food Display Items (on center display table or in baskets on the individual tables):

Almonds, pistachios

Parsley, mint, sage, cinnamon

Olives, dates, grapes

Fava, garbanzo beans

Cucumber, lemon, orange

Garlic, onions, horseradish

Turnips, beets, lettuce, dandelion

Honey, "locust" (candy bugs)

Dark and unleavened bread

Dried fish, milk

Craft Supplies and Instructions:

Mancala Game Craft

Supplies

(A complete game needs one egg carton, two small cups and 48 beans, beads, etc.)

- Cardboard egg carton (dozen size)
- Small 4-ounce cups (two for each game made)
- Markers, stickers, or paints to decorate the egg cartons (if desired)
- 48 beans, beads, tiny rocks, or marbles per game

Directions

Object: To collect the most beans/beads in your *mancala* (cup)

Game set-up: Place four beans/beads in each "egg." Do not put any in the cups. Place egg carton between two players, with the *mancalas* (cups) to the left and the right of the egg carton. Each player "owns" the *mancala* (cup) on his right.

Play: Player 1 starts by scooping all the beans/beads from one of his eggs or from one of his opponent's eggs. Then he drops one bean/bead into the next egg on the right, one bead into the next bowl on the right, continuing counterclockwise, including his own *mancala* (cup) until there are no more beans/beads in his hand. Do not drop a bean/bead into the opponent's *mancala,* skip and continue around the egg carton. Players take turns moving. At the end of the game, the player with the most beans/beads in their own *mancala* wins.

Knucklebones Game Craft

Supplies
(Real animal bones were used for this game when Jesus was a boy.)
- Air dried clay

Directions

Make four clay "bones" — one with a flat side, one with a concave (curved or rounded inside) side, one with a convex (curved or rounded outside) side and one with a twisted side.

Instructions to Play
Hold four "bones" in your hand, toss them up, flip your hand over and try to catch them on the back of your hand. The winner is the one who can catch the most in the fewest tries. (This is similar to Jacks today.)

Refreshments:
Coffee, mint tea, and lemonade
Biscuits or pita bread cut into pieces, served warm with honey or cinnamon
"Locust" snacks (candy gummy bugs)

Project Checklist

_____

_____

_____

_____

_____

_____

_____

_____

_____

_____

_____

_____

_____

_____

_____

_____

_____

_____

_____

11. LENT

Objective:

To give families an opportunity to pray together in the season of Lent, and to provide children with a "good deed" craft and a learning activity on the Passion of Christ.

Supplies Needed:

For Prayer (a set for each table):

- Clear bowls of water, large enough to submerge an adult hand
- Lumps of clay
- Mustard seeds in a bowl
- Sand in a flat container
- White candles and matches
- Bible

Setting:

Tables and chairs in one area. At the center of each table is a bowl of water, a fist-size piece of soft clay, a flat container of sand (aluminum pan works well), a white candle, and several mustard seeds.

A series of "stations" each with a descriptive sign and symbol (on a small paper "panel") depicting the events of Holy Week. At each of the 13 stations, the families will pick up a small panel to glue onto their "yardstick" craft.

If desired, another table could have an additional craft designed to help remember to do "good deeds" during the season.

Activity Summary:

Families share prayer and complete a Passion "time line" with symbols/Scripture passages, followed by the "good deed" craft.

Prayer Script:

Lenten Family Gathering

(Round tables are covered with purple tablecloths; the center of each table has sand, a white candle, a lump of clay, some mustard seeds, and a clear bowl of water. You may wish to use one reader or several.)

Reader #1: Welcome to our Lenten Family Gathering. It is always our intention that our short time together will provide your family with a deeper understanding of our Church seasons; and will give your children some concrete ways to learn about their faith. For our prayer today, we will be using the symbols in the center of each table. We have water … clay … sand … a white candle … and some mustard seeds. Lent is the time we try especially hard to become more like Jesus.

Reader #2: When we were baptized, we joined God's family. He claimed us as His own. In Lent, we try to live our lives to please God. No matter how young or old we are, there are small things or large things that we try to do every day to remember that we belong to God, we are His Family.

We invite you now to pass the bowl of water around the table. Put your hands deep into the bowl, and feel the water covering your hands. Like the water covering our hands, the love of God covers us and is all around us. When you take your hand out of the water, make the Sign of the Cross on your forehead. Remember, you are claimed by God. You belong to God, and He Loves You.

Reader #3: A reading from the book of Jeremiah, chapter 18:

"The word that came to Jeremiah from the LORD: 'Arise and go down to the potter's house, and there I will let you hear my words.' So I went down to the potter's house, and there he was working at his wheel. And the vessel he was making of clay was spoiled in the potter's hand, and he reworked it into another vessel, as it seemed good to the potter to do. Then the word of the LORD came to me: '… Behold, like the clay in the potter's hand, so are you in my hand.'"

We ask that you now take the clay from the center of your tables, and break off a piece. Close your eyes a moment, and think that God is holding you in his hands, and you are the clay He is shaping and reshaping. Form something with the clay. Notice, as the clay is soft, you can make something from it. If clay becomes too hard, it can break into little pieces. We need to always be open to how God wants to shape our lives.

Reader #4: Also in the center of your tables are small bowls of seeds and a layer of sand. Remember, in Scripture it says that the mustard seed is the smallest of all seeds, and when planted, it grows into the largest of all bushes. Take a seed and see how very small it is. We are told that if we have faith the size of this seed, God can work wonders with us. This Lent, remember that every good deed you do will help your faith to grow.

Now we have the sand on your table. Write something — anything — on the sand and then have someone else at the table smooth it over. We know that our sins are wiped clean by Jesus. We need to confess our sins, like writing in the sand, and God smoothes them over. He forgives us when we ask for it.

Reader #1: Finally on your tables is an unlit candle. We ask for an adult, at this time, to light the candle. Light is what Jesus says He is to us … "I am the Light of the world; he who follows me will not walk in darkness." Remember, this Lent, and in every day ahead, to always FOLLOW THE LIGHT OF JESUS. He will lead the way.

At this time, we would like to explain our projects for today. Each table has purple beads, a white pipe cleaner decorated with a butterfly, a cross, and some markers. Lent is a time of changing — much like a caterpillar changes from something that crawls on the ground, to something very beautiful that flies in the sky. We have a project to help you remember this each day of Lent.

Color your caterpillar (white pipe cleaner) in stripes with markers. Put a cross on the bottom of it. String six purple beads. Everyday in Lent, with every good deed you do, you are to move one bead up to the top. The next day, you push them down, and start all over.

We have a magnet on the back of the butterfly. Put this on your refrigerator, and every day see how you are doing with pushing your beads to the top.

In the next room, we have 13 stations. At each station, stop and think a few minutes about the event in Jesus' life that the Scripture and symbol show. Then, take one picture from the basket at each table. When you have gone to all the stations, come to the "glue table" where you will get a purple yardstick to place your pictures. Why do you think we are using a yardstick? Yardsticks measure growth. Lent is a time set aside for all of us to grow closer to Jesus. Why is it purple? Purple is the color of our Church season. Take time today to glue the pictures in the right order, remembering always how much we are loved by Jesus.

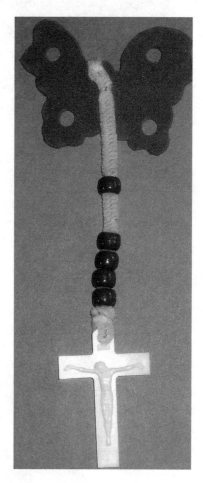

Craft Instructions and Supplies:

Caterpillar/Butterfly craft

Supplies
- White pipe cleaners
- Purple beads
- Strip of magnet
- Markers
- Small crosses to tie onto end of pipe cleaners
- Butterflies (foam, stickers, or cut out construction or wrapping paper)

Directions
Color the white pipe cleaner in stripes with markers.
Attach the cross at the bottom of the pipe cleaner.
String six purple beads on the pipe cleaner from the top.
Attach a butterfly on the top of the caterpillar.
Glue a small piece of a magnet on the back of the butterfly.

Yardstick Craft

Supplies

- One yardstick for each child, painted purple
- 13 sketches and Scripture verses of Holy Week events (see pages 115–116)
- Small twig crosses
- Small white flower (picture or artificial)
- Scripture verse and sketch (or symbol) for station centerpieces

Directions

Glue sketches in right order on yardstick.

Glue twig cross to the left end.

Glue white flower to the right end.

Refreshments:

A variety of breads and butter

Juice and coffee

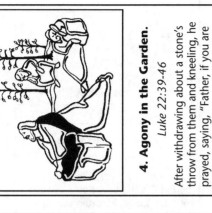

1. Triumphant entry into Jerusalem.
Matthew 21:1-11

The crowds preceding him and those following kept crying out and saying,

"Hosanna to the Son of David, blessed is he who comes in the name of the Lord; Hosanna in the highest."

2. Washing of the disciples' feet.

John 13:1-20

Then he poured water into a basin and began to wash the disciples' feet and dry them with the towel around his waist.

3. Last Supper.
Matthew 26:1-29

While they were eating, Jesus took the bread, said the blessing, broke it, and giving it to his disciples said, "Take and eat; this is my body." Then he took a cup, gave thanks, and gave it to them, saying, "Drink from it, all of you, for this is my blood of the covenant, which will be shed on behalf of many for the forgiveness of sins."

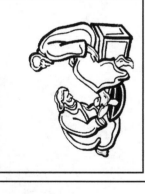

4. Agony in the Garden.
Luke 22:39-46

After withdrawing about a stone's throw from them and kneeling, he prayed, saying, "Father, if you are willing, take this cup away from me; still, not my will but yours be done."

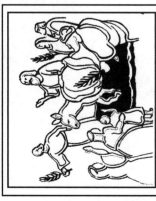

5. Judas Betrays Jesus.
Mark 14:43-50

Then, while he was still speaking, Judas, one of the Twelve, arrived, accompanied by a crowd with swords and clubs...His betrayer had arranged a signal with them, saying, "The man I shall kiss is the one; arrest him and lead him away securely."

6. Peter's Denial.
Matthew 26:69-75

"I do not know the man." And immediately a cock crowed. Then Peter remembered the word that Jesus had spoken: "Before the cock crows you will deny me three times." He went out and began to weep bitterly.

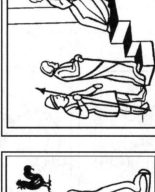

7. Jesus before Pilate.
Matthew 27:1-2

They bound him, led him away, and handed him over to Pilate, the governor.

8. Crown of Thorns.
John 19:2-3

And the soldiers wove a crown out of thorns and placed it on his head, and clothed him in a purple cloak, and they came to him and said, "Hail, King of the Jews!" And they struck him repeatedly.

9. Carrying the Cross.

John 19:17

So they took Jesus, and carrying the Cross himself he went out to what is called the Place of the Skull, in Hebrew, Golgotha.

10. Crucifixion.

John 19:25-30

When Jesus saw his mother and the disciple there whom he loved, he said to his mother, "Woman, behold, your son." Then he said to the disciple, "Behold, your mother." And bowing his head, he handed over the spirit.

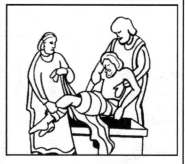

11. Burial of Jesus.

John 19:39-42

They took the body of Jesus and bound it with burial cloths along with the spices, according to the Jewish burial custom.

12. Empty Tomb.

Mark 16:1-2

When the Sabbath was over, Mary Magdalene, Mary, the mother of James, and Salome bought spices so that they might go and anoint him.

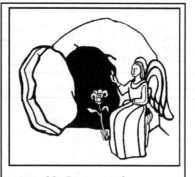

13. Resurrection.

Mark 16:4-8

On entering the tomb, they saw a young man sitting on the right side, clothed in a white robe, and they were utterly amazed. He said to them, "Do not be amazed! You seek Jesus of Nazareth, the crucified. He has been raised; he is not here."

12. HOLY WEEK FAMILY GATHERING

Objective:

To reflect on the events of Holy Week and to make bread as a symbol of Christ.

Setting:

A front table is covered in white and is empty except for a crucifix. The tables for the families are centered with a square of purple or gold (felt, construction paper, etc.), and each of these holds an item that one child will bring up during the reading. One tray per table holds all the measured ingredients for the bread making. Access to an oven is needed unless the bread is to be sent home to be baked. Craft and refreshment tables are prepared and covered until after the bread-making activity.

Activity Summary:

Families listen to the Holy Week story and participate by bringing items up and placing them on the table next to the crucifix. Then each table mixes the ingredients for bread while drawing a parallel to Jesus. While the bread bakes (if not to be divided and sent home with the families), the children prepare a "simple banner" to use in the Palm Sunday procession.

Prayer Supplies:

- Crucifix
- White tablecloth
- Purple squares (paper, cloth)
- Lamb's wool
- Cup and a plate with bread
- Dish of coins
- Red robe or cloth
- Crown
- Three nails
- Sign saying, "King of the Jews"
- White cloth
- Cloves or cinnamon sticks
- A rock and an artificial lily

Holy Week Family Gathering

Script:

Welcome to our Family Gathering focusing on the coming events of Holy Week. Today we will begin with a Scripture reading. When we come to the quote on your table, please bring up your object and place it on the front table.

1. "Here is the Lamb of God, who takes away the sin of the world." (lamb's wool)

2. "Then Jesus took the bread, said the blessing, and broke it, saying, "This is my body, which will be given for you; do this in memory of me." (cup and plate with bread)

3. "Then one of the twelve who was called Judas went to the chief priests and said what will you give me if I betray Him to you?" (dish of gold coins)

4. "They stripped him and put a scarlet robe on Him." (red robe or piece of cloth)

5. "After twisting some thorns into a crown, they put it on His head." (crown)

6. "Jesus was nailed to the cross." (three nails, sign saying, "King of the Jews")

7. "After Jesus died on the cross, His body was wrapped in linen cloths. The women brought spices to anoint His body." (linen cloths and spices)

8. "A great rock was rolled in front of the tomb." (rock)

9. "At daybreak on the first day of the week, they went to the tomb. They found the stone rolled away and did not find the body of Jesus. He is risen!" (a lily)

These are the scriptural words that tell the story of Jesus' Passion. The Easter message of New Life may also be remembered by simply making bread…

Each ingredient we use speaks to us of the meaning of Christ's Death and Resurrection. This recipe also calls us to a deeper understanding of discipleship. We'd like each table to prepare the bread together, then divide it into a loaf for each family to take home. Please have one person at each table be the READER of the description of each item as you mix the bread dough together. As the parents are dividing up the bread dough to take home, or waiting while we bake it, we invite the children to make a banner to wave in the Palm Sunday Procession. Boys and girls, what are we remembering when we walk around the Church on Palm Sunday? Yes! Jesus' ride into Jerusalem on a donkey! This is the Sunday in our Church year when we receive palms in Church that have been blessed with holy water. These palms remind us of this Holy Week all year long.

Script for each table for bread making: (Copies on each table.)

Easter Family Bread

The Easter message of new life in the Resurrection may be remembered by simply baking bread.

Each ingredient we use speaks to us of the meaning of Christ's Death and Resurrection. This recipe also calls us to a deeper understanding of discipleship.

Flour: Wheat is made up of many individual grains. Grain has to be crushed together, all the little seeds broken and changed to become flour. This is like all of us. Jesus wants all of us to be changed, to die to our own ways of doing things … of being separate, to become one body. The Church is like "flour." It is One Body, made up of many different parts working together.

We have two types of flour here. The colors may be different, just as there are different types of people, but they come together to make something better than they are alone.

(Mix together the types of flour and stir well.)

Salt: The Resurrection of Jesus is the SALT of our world. Salt preserves food. Salt keeps food from spoiling. Believing in Jesus saves us. In Scripture, we are told that we are to be the "salt of the world." Who has tasted chips or pretzels without salt? They do not have much taste! If we are to be "salt" for the world, we need to do good works and flavor the world with kindness.

(Mix the salt with the flour and stir.)

Baking soda and cream of tartar: These items are like "yeast" mentioned in the Bible. They make the bread rise. When bread dough rises, it becomes totally different. It changes everything. Jesus is like "yeast" to us. He wants to "bubble up" in our life and change us by His Love for us.

(Mix the baking soda and cream of tartar with the flour and salt.)

Sugar or honey: The sweetness of honey or sugar is what makes the yeast or the baking soda rise. Without the sweetener, the bread would stay flat — it wouldn't be changed. The Resurrection of Jesus is the sweetest message of all. It is what makes our faith come alive.

Milk: Milk is very important for babies and children to grow. It is all they need in the first few months of their lives. Jesus is what we need to help us grow. Just as babies depend on milk alone when they are very tiny and need so much care, we need to depend like that on Jesus. Our belief in the Resurrection is what nourishes us and "keeps us going."

Oil: Oil in bread gives it strength. It makes it more filling because it is heavier. When we are baptized, the priest blesses our hearts and our heads with oil to give us the strength to live as a Christian. When we are confirmed, oil is again used as a symbol of strength. Oil in bread nourishes us and keeps us from being hungry for things that are not good for us in our world.

(Mix the sugar or honey, oil, and the milk into the dry ingredients)

Spices, raisins, and fruit: We know from the Bible that Christians live "fruitful" lives and flavor our world with sweetness!

Bread Supplies for Each Table:

- 6 cups flour (any combination of white, whole wheat, corn meal, each in a separate container)
- 1 tsp salt
- 1 tsp baking soda
- 1 tsp cream of tartar
- 1 tsp sugar or honey
- 2 cups milk
- 2T oil
- 1 tsp cinnamon or nutmeg
- Small amount of raisins
- Large bowl
- Plastic gloves
- Mixing bowl

Craft Supplies and Instructions:

Palm Sunday Procession Banner Craft

Supplies

- Balloon sticks or small paper plates
- Variety of colors of thin ribbon
- Markers, paper, or pictures of Jesus
- Hole punch
- Tape, glue, and glue applicators (if using the pictures of Jesus)

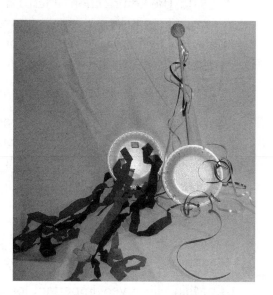

Directions

If using a paper plate, hole punch around the rim of the plate.

Thread ribbons (10" to 12"long) through the holes and knot.

Draw or glue in the center of the plate a picture of Jesus.

If using a balloon stick, tie or tape six or seven ribbons onto the end or draw a picture of Jesus and tape it on the end of the stick.

Refreshments:

Hot cross buns or pretzel knots (symbols of a cross and praying arms)

Beverages

13. PENTECOST

Objective:

To link the events of Pentecost with the gifts of the Holy Spirit and the parts of the Church.

Setting:

Tables for the group are facing a wall to which a large church outline and a large outline of a gift box are taped. An open space should be left, large enough to accommodate the number of children who will come and sit in front of the speaker. Each table has a clue envelope, paper, markers, and tape. Eight tables have a puzzle piece, and one has a bow. One or more pictures of church windows, taped over mirrors or mirror paper, can be hung near the exit.

A separate table with the refreshments (birthday cake, coffee, juice) is set apart and covered to be served after the presentation. The decorations are birthday themed and as festive as the budget allows (plates, napkins, streamers, balloons, centerpieces).

Floor fans are positioned behind or next to the speaker, and are aimed at the space where the children sit on the floor. A CD or tape player is nearby to play sound effects of strong winds (if desired and available).

Activity Summary:

Parents gather at tables, and the children come up and sit on floor in front of the speakers for a demonstration on the Pentecost Scripture passages (1 to 4 readers). After the skit, the children join their parents at table for birthday cake, and the narration continues with a presentation on the Holy Spirit. A short discussion follows on the gifts of the Holy Spirit, with several engaging activities for the families. Then the speaker leads a riddle about objects found in the church, and children bring up pictures (inside clue envelopes) and add those to the church shape. The craft is a kite that can be made on site or taken home to complete.

Script Supplies:

- A large (3 to 4 feet tall) black outline of a church shape painted onto paper, and a similar Holy Spirit Gift Box shape with the puzzle shapes (that are on the tables) traced within it (bulletin board paper, butcher paper, heavy wrapping paper, or black tape outlined on a blank wall works to form an outline).
- Pentecost "flames": Tape together at one end a "bunch" — five or six 2-foot pieces of red, yellow, and orange crepe paper to wave over the heads of the children.
- Red, yellow, and orange helium balloons to release during the Pentecost Scripture (if desired — not really necessary!)
- Room fans and a CD or tape player with sound effects of strong winds

- A "window" flap that can be lifted to reveal a mirror. It is a picture of a stained glass window that can be placed next to the door where the families exit or by itself on a smaller church. Having two at different heights is also a nice touch to accommodate both adults and small children.

On each table:
- A large manila envelope with a clue describing an item found in the church printed on the outside and a picture of that item inside.
- Puzzle pieces for the Holy Spirit Gift Box outline made of heavy paper, craft foam, or cardboard, with one of the gifts of the Holy Spirit written on it (Wisdom, Understanding, Right Judgment, Courage, Knowledge, Reverence, Wonder and Awe)
- One large bow to stick on the Holy Spirit Gift Box
- Paper and markers for writing our own gifts to share with the church.
- Tape or removable putty
- At least one inflated red balloon and one not blown up
- Materials for making a kite

Script: (Four Readers)

A: Welcome to our Pentecost Family Gathering! We'd like to begin with all the children gathered in front of me on the floor. Pentecost is a word that needs a little more explanation for young children — so we will "demonstrate" what it means.

A reading from Acts, Chapter 2. *(Speaking slowly and deliberately)*

A: When Pentecost day came around, they had all met in one room …

B: … when they heard what sounded like a powerful wind from Heaven, the noise of which filled the entire house in which they were sitting …

(Helpers A and D turn on the fans and the "wind" tape, let them roar for a minute, then turn them off before the next speaker resumes.)

C: … and something happened to them that seemed like tongues of fire … these separated and came to rest on the head of each of them …

(All helpers wave yellow, red, and orange crepe paper bundles [about 2-foot-long pieces tied together] over the children's heads — or release a few red, yellow, and orange helium balloons.)

D: They were all filled with the Holy Spirit, and began to speak foreign languages as the Spirit gave them the gift of speech.

A: Now, we would like all the children to "speak in a foreign language" as you go back and join your parents.

(Pause while children move back to their families.)

What we just learned about is considered the "birthday of the Church."

From the Holy Spirit coming down … in the mighty wind … in the flames … in the sudden ability to speak foreign languages … God, through the actions of the Holy Spirit, gave us the Church!

We can say we are celebrating the birthday of the Church on Pentecost!

You are invited to enjoy some birthday cake, juice, and coffee.

(After a few minutes, when everyone has picked up their refreshments and returned to their seats, the speaker can resume.)

A: Now, as you can see on the wall, we are going to be talking this morning about Church and the Holy Spirit.

A symbol of the Holy Spirit is a balloon. Filled with air, the balloon has shape. It moves around, flies with the wind, gives joy to people, etc. We don't see the air — we don't see the Holy Spirit — but it makes all the difference!

An empty balloon, like this one, is useless. It has no purpose, unless you fill it with air. Our lives need the movement of the Holy Spirit to give us purpose.

Another example of something moved by the wind is a kite. When we are finished in here, we invite you to take a few minutes and make a kite to take home. A kite can remind us of the Holy Spirit. It "moves along" with the wind — like we move along in our lives guided by the Holy Spirit.

In the Bible, we read of seven very special gifts — the gifts of the Holy Spirit. These seven gifts are a wonderful present given to all of us to help us each day of our life.

When we use these gifts of the Holy Spirit, our Church is at its best. God wants us to use this wonderful present — these gifts of the Holy Spirit — to do His work in the world. Do you think God has a lot of work to do in our world? That is why He has given us the seven gifts of the Holy Spirit!

Each table has a part of this present from God. One table has the bow to go on top of the present.

Could we have one child from each table bring up the puzzle piece? You can see it is a very large gift box, so it needs a bow on top, too.

(Children bring up the pieces of the Holy Spirit puzzle and the bow, placing them in position on an outline of a gift with the puzzle shapes drawn in it.)

Now, some of these words are hard to understand. We ask you now to talk together with those at your tables about what one of those gifts of the Holy Spirit means. There are paper and markers so that you can draw or write an example of how to use this gift. When your table is done, come up and tape these examples around our picture of the church.

Let us share some examples of how we can use these special gifts.

We know from these examples that God needs us to use these wonderful gifts because we are the Church. All of us together are the Church.

What else do we know about the inside of the Church? Each table has an envelope with some part of the Church in it.

Pentecost

I will read a clue and someone from the table with that envelope can give us the answer and bring the picture inside the envelope up and place it on the church sketch on the wall.

Clues on the outside of the envelopes (see page 128 for labels)**:**

1. I hold the gifts of my Church family, given with a happy heart, to help meet the needs of the Church and take care of the poor. What am I?
2. I am the "Good News!" What am I?
3. I hold the precious Blood of Christ. Many people drink from me as *one.* What am I? My partner holds the Body of Christ. What is it called?
4. I am wet. There are three steps down, and three steps up. I give "new life" to all who enter me. What am I?
5. You see me in every Catholic Church and in most all Christian churches. I am created from many different materials — gold, wood, pottery. What am I?
6. I am beautifully designed, because I "hold" Jesus. What am I?
7. I am a very special place in every Catholic Church. People come in to me sometimes burdened and sad. They leave knowing the forgiveness of God. What am I?
8. People speak the Word of God from me. What am I?
9. I am the sacred place where bread and wine are changed to be the Body and Blood of Jesus. What am I?
10. I bring "Light" to our church after there have been two days of darkness. I am used at every Baptism for one year, beginning at the Easter Vigil. What am I?
11. There are fifteen of me. We help people remember and pray the story of Jesus' death and resurrection. What are we?
12. I am a little cupboard that holds holy oils that the priest uses to bless the sick. What am I?

Answers (pictures provided on pages 129-130)**:**

1. Gift basket
2. Lectionary
3. Chalice and paten
4. Baptismal font
5. Crucifix or Cross
6. Tabernacle
7. Confessional
8. Ambo
9. Altar
10. Easter Candle
11. Stations of the Cross
12. Ambry

Our last riddle is to find one of the most important parts of our Church. As you leave, look behind the stained glass window for the answer.

(A mirror or mirror paper is behind a drawing of a stained glass window, taped to the wall forming a flap that can be lifted saying: "You are an important part of the Church!")

Kite Craft Supplies and Instructions:

Supplies

- White or red lunch bags
- Markers or crayons
- String (three pieces each about three inches long, and a longer piece for each kite)
- Scissors
- Wire loops approximately three inches in diameter

Directions

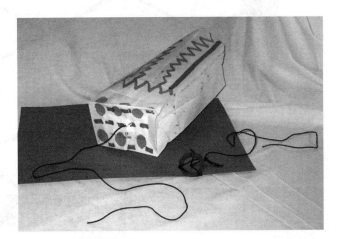

Cut a small hole into the bottom of the lunch bag.

Decorate the bag with markers.

Form wire into a circle larger than the hole in the bag.

Tie three strings to the wire circle; tie the other ends together in a knot.

Put the wire loop into the bag.

Pull the three short strings out through the hole.

Attach a longer string to the three-string knot, long enough to fly it.

Refreshments:

Large sheet cake decorated in birthday theme ("Happy Birthday to our Church!" for example) or trays of decorated cupcakes. Coffee, tea, and juice or lemonade. Paper goods in either red or a birthday theme.

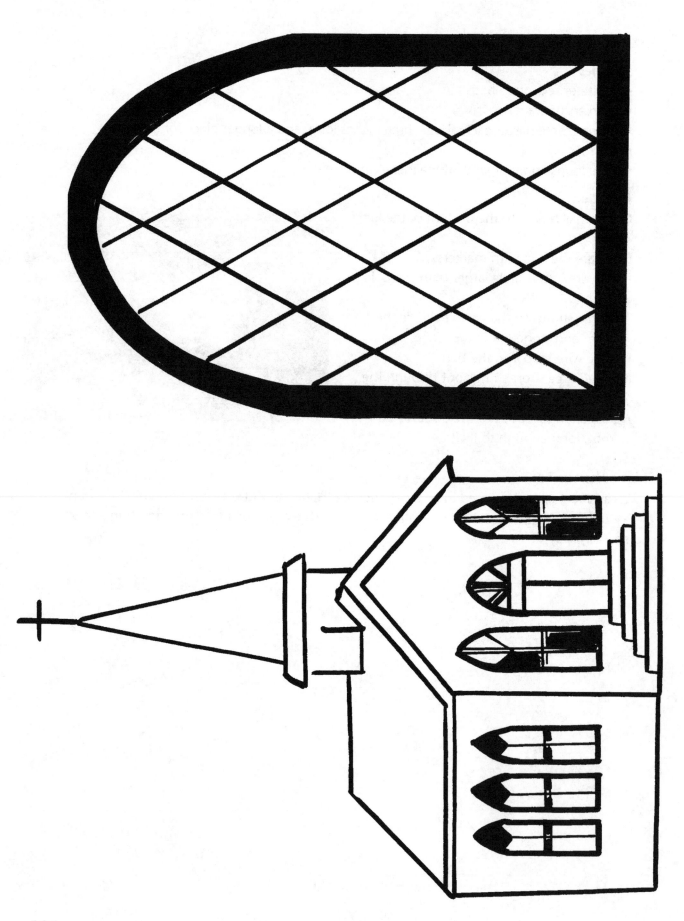

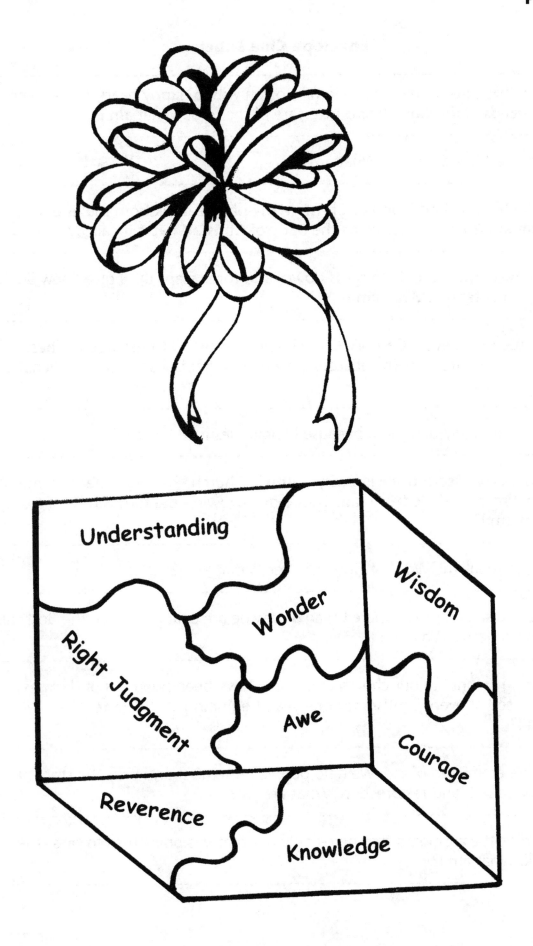

Envelope Clue Labels

1. I hold the gifts of my Church family, given with a happy heart, to help meet the needs of the Church and take care of the poor. What am I?

2. I am the "Good News!" What am I?

3. I hold the precious Blood of Christ. Many people drink from me as one. What am I? My partner holds the Body of Christ. What is it called?

4. I am wet. There are three steps down, and three steps up. I give "new life" to all who enter me. What am I?

5. You see me in every Catholic Church and in most all Christian churches. I am created from many different materials — gold, wood, pottery. What am I?

6. I am beautifully designed, because I "hold" Jesus. What am I?

7. I am a very special place in every Catholic Church. People come in to me sometimes burdened and sad. They leave knowing the forgiveness of God. What am I?

8. People speak the Word of God from me. What am I?

9. I am the sacred place where bread and wine are changed to be the Body and Blood of Jesus. What am I?

10. I bring "Light" to our church after there have been two days of darkness. I am used at every Baptism for one year, beginning at the Easter Vigil. What am I?

11. There are fifteen of me. We help people remember and pray the story of Jesus' death and resurrection. What are we?

12. I am a little cupboard that holds holy oils that the priest uses to bless the sick. What am I?

1. Gift basket

2. Lectionary

3. Chalice and paten

4. Baptismal font

5. Crucifix or Cross

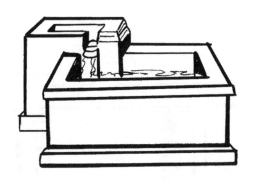

6. Tabernacle

7. Confessional

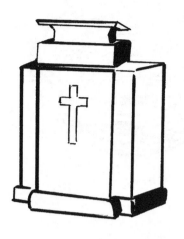

8. Ambo

9. Altar

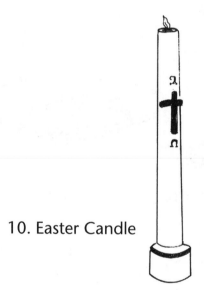

10. Easter Candle

11. Stations of the Cross

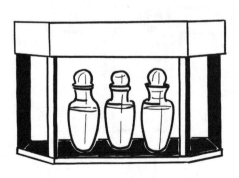

12. Ambry

14. SACRAMENTS OF INITIATION

Objective:

To familiarize young children and their parents with the symbols and the rites of Baptism, Eucharist, and Confirmation.

Activity Summary:

The children and their parents move from one sacrament setting to another, participating in either role-play or a ritual to explain the meaning of the sacrament. At each of the three areas, they pick up small drawings of the symbols of the sacraments, which they use to make the craft at the end. The craft is a small three-dimensional church, with the sacrament symbols "popping out" from within.

Setting and Items Needed for Sacrament Stations:

Four activity areas (spaced as far apart as possible) arranged as follows:

— The Eucharist Station
  - Table and chairs
  - Simple table cover and several candles
  - Small juice cups
  - Center loaf of bread
  - Basin of water
  - Towel
— The Baptism Station
  - Basin of water
  - White garment
  - Fragrant oil
  - Candle
  - A doll
  - Props for role-play — purse, hat and/or scarf for the Mother and Godmother; ties for the Father and the Godfather
— The Confirmation Station
  - Red tablecloth
  - Oil
  - Dove
  - Arrangement of oils, signs, and symbols as described.
  - Bishop's mitre (cardboard) and staff

Sacraments of Initiation

- On a side table, with a variation in heights (by placing small boxes underneath a table cover) are many different types of oil with explanations as to their use: Baby oil, furniture polishing oil, "3-in-One engine oil," motor oil, lamp oil, cooking oil, fragrance oil, etc. In addition there are symbols: wealth (bowl of "gold" coins); strength (small hand weight — barbell); royalty (crown); cleansing (cleaning cloth); beautifying (mirror); nourishment (cooking pan); healing (medicinal ointment); light (small lamp); and "nonfriction" "smooth engine running" (child's truck).
- Small signs may be prepared for this display as follows:

  wealth

  light

  cooking

  healing, cleansing, and beautifying

  nourishment and taste

  royalty

  stops friction

  strength

— Craft table is the fourth area.

Baptism Script and Action:

(Have on a table: A tablecloth; a large center candle [if possible, an old Paschal candle]; a "baptism candle"; a white garment; a little fragrant oil; a bowl of water; and a towel.)

A box of props (the baby doll included) for the children to wear (previously listed).

Today we are going to learn about a very important celebration! You may have seen a picture of yourself when you were a baby and you and your family celebrated your Baptism. Sacraments are special moments in your life when you meet God in a new way, and know how much He loves you. Baptism is the first sacrament someone experiences. In Baptism, you become a child of God. You join a new family, the Christian family. Everyone who loves Jesus is one family! I'm going to need your help. Who wants to be the Mom, the Dad, or the Godparents?

(Roles are given and the children receive the appropriate props.)

Catechist (as the priest, looking at the "parents" who are holding the "baby"): What name do you give your child?

Parents answer. (They select a name before skit begins.)

"Priest":   What do you ask of God's Church for your child?

Parents answer.

"Priest":   You have asked that your child be baptized. By doing this, you accept the responsibility to raise him/her as Jesus taught us — to teach him/her to love God, and love others.

"Priest":   Do you understand this responsibility?

Parents answer.

"Priest" (*Turning to Godparents*): Are you willing to help these parents to raise this child to be like Jesus?

Godparents answer.

"Priest":   Our Church welcomes you! I ask you now to trace the Sign of the Cross on your baby's forehead, and on each other. I ask the entire community gathered here to celebrate with us today, to sign your neighbor with the Sign of the Cross. By doing this, we remember that each one of us has been claimed by Jesus and we belong to Him.

(*Everyone signs each other.*)

"Priest":   I'm going to put a little oil on the heart of your baby, as a sign of strengthening your child to live as a Christian.

("*Priest*" *is looking up while holding the clear bowl filled with water and praying that God will bless the water and make it holy.*)

"Priest" (*looking at the parents and the Godparents, and inviting everyone in the "congregation" to respond together*): Do you believe in God the Father, Jesus, His Son, and the Holy Spirit?

(*With the parents holding the baby, and the Godparents touching him/her also, the "Priest" baptizes the baby*): (Name) I baptize you in the name of the Father, and of the Son, and of the Holy Spirit.

"Priest":   I anoint you with sweet smelling oil. May you know the sweetness of the Christian life.

"Priest":   This white garment is a sign that you are now a new creation.

(*Parents put on the white garment.*)

"Priest":   Receive the Light of Christ. Always walk as a Child of the Light, following the way of Jesus.

"Priest":   Let us welcome our new Christian!

("*Congregation*" *claps.*)

(*Catechist gives all the children the symbols of the sacrament to use in making their craft after they have completed the three sacrament areas.*)

Eucharist Script and Action:

Jesus Eats with All Types of People

In the Bible, we hear many stories of Jesus eating and drinking with people. All different types of people! Rich, poor, important people or strangers. Jesus loved everyone just the same. He taught many lessons when eating food with His friends. While they ate, Jesus talked to them about God's love and forgiveness.

As followers of Jesus, we also listen to His stories and share a meal together with Him by being together at Mass and sharing the Communion Bread and Wine. Jesus is with us now just as much as He once was with His friends many years ago. The very last meal that Jesus shared with His friends on Earth tells us why.

The Last Supper

The night before Jesus died was a special feast for the Jews. It was the time when they remembered together the great moment in their history when God saved them from slavery in Egypt. This special feast is called Passover. Just as God saved the Jews so many years ago, He saves us through the love of Jesus.

When Jesus celebrated the Passover with His closest friends, He taught them how important it is to serve each other. He took water and a towel and washed the feet of each of His disciples. When Jesus lived, the roads were very dusty and hot. So, when guests came to dinner, there were servants to wash the feet of company. By Jesus taking water and washing His disciples' feet, He taught them to serve others. This lesson is for us today. We need to help others like Jesus. Now, I am going to go around the table, and wash and dry your hands.

On that night, Jesus also used a new symbol to show His friends that He was giving His life for them. He took a loaf of bread and broke it and shared it. When it was broken, shared, and eaten, it became part of their bodies. In just this way Jesus gives Himself to us. Because He gave His life for us, He is no longer separate and apart from His friends. He gives Himself to us. He becomes part of us.

This is what Jesus meant when He took bread, broke it, and said:

"This is my body which is given for you. Do this in remembrance of me." (Luke 22:19)

This is what the priest means at Mass when he takes the host and says:

"Take this all of you and eat it: This is my body which will be given up for you."

Now, let us share this one loaf of bread by taking a piece and passing it on to your neighbor.

At the Last Supper, Jesus also took a cup of wine. He shared this with his friends saying:

"This cup which is poured out for you is the new covenant in my blood." (Luke 22:20)

At Mass the priest takes wine and says:

"Take this, all of you, and drink from it:
This is the cup of my blood,
the blood of the new and everlasting covenant.
It will be shed for you and for many
so that sins may be forgiven.
Do this in memory of me."

Jesus is telling His friends through the wine the same thing that He has already said with the bread. His death on the cross brings us much closer to Him and to one another. He is now going to live with us and in us. Now, from this one pitcher, we will pour out juice for each of us to share as we remember Jesus and all the Love He has for us. Let us remember also to love and serve each other, as Jesus asks us to do.

(Catechist gives the children the sacrament symbols to use in making their craft.)

Confirmation Script and Action:

Welcome to the sacrament of Confirmation! Look around at all these oils! As you can see, oil is very important in many ways. How is it used in the sacrament of Confirmation? Oil is a symbol of the Holy Spirit anointing us — giving us special gifts that will help us live better lives. Gifts like courage, knowledge, and understanding.

Has anyone had a brother or sister who was confirmed? What do you remember about it?

Confirmation is like the second half of the sacrament of Baptism. When you were baptized, the Holy Spirit was given to you, and you became part of God's family. Confirmation is saying "Yes" to the Holy Spirit to give you all special gifts so that your life will be more like Jesus.

A bishop, wearing a tall hat called a mitre, and a staff, comes to our church once a year, and he uses oil to mark the Sign of the Cross on the forehead of the person to be confirmed. Let's look at these types of oil and think about each one and what it does.

In the Bible, oil is mentioned many times. It is a sign of someone very wealthy! (Hold up coins.) When someone had a lot of oil in their home, they would be well fed (hold pan up). They could keep their lights burning — as you know, people didn't have electric lamps, they had oil-burning lamps (hold up lamp). Also, oil was important in cleaning (hold up cleaning cloth); in making skin healthy, smooth, and beautiful (hold up ointment and mirror). Oil is also able to keep engines, and all types of machines running smoothly (hold up toy truck). And boys and girls, oil was used to make people strong.

Long ago, when athletes competed in wrestling or races, their trainers would rub their muscles with oil to strengthen them (hold up barbell). Also, in the time of Jesus, when someone was made a King, they would anoint his head, pour oil over his head. We have a crown here to show you that oil was meant for royalty (hold up crown). When we see all the uses of oil we can understand why it is used in the sacrament of Confirmation. I will now dip my finger in this sweet smelling oil and mark you with the Sign of the Cross on your forehead. The oil used at Confirmation smells very sweet — this helps us remember that our lives should have a goodness or sweetness about them.

To end our time learning about this sacrament, we remember that when Jesus first gave the Holy Spirit to His disciples, He said "Peace be with you." Like we do each week in Church, let us now give a sign of peace to each other.

(Catechist gives the children the sacrament symbols to use in making their craft.)

Refreshments:

Three signs that read: Baptism, Eucharist, and Confirmation
Baptism area refreshment table: Pitchers of water, white angel food cake, and whipped topping
Eucharist area: Pitcher of grape juice, loaf of homemade bread cut in small pieces
Confirmation: Large bowl of fruit

Sacraments of Initiation Craft:

Supplies *(for each)*

- Black line drawing of church (template on page 137)
- Black line clip art of Baptism, Eucharist, and Confirmation (two each) (templates on page 138)
- Dry floral foam or Styrofoam, cut into 2.5" squares, 1.25" thick
- Three colored craft sticks
- Large colored paper clips
- Clear tape
- Markers or crayons

Directions

Color in the church and the sacrament pictures.

Cut out four churches in one long strip; the sacraments individually.

Glue or tape the church strip around the foam square.

Tape one paper clip securely to each craft stick.

Gently push the sticks into the foam.

Slip the sacrament pictures into the clips, back to back, in pairs.

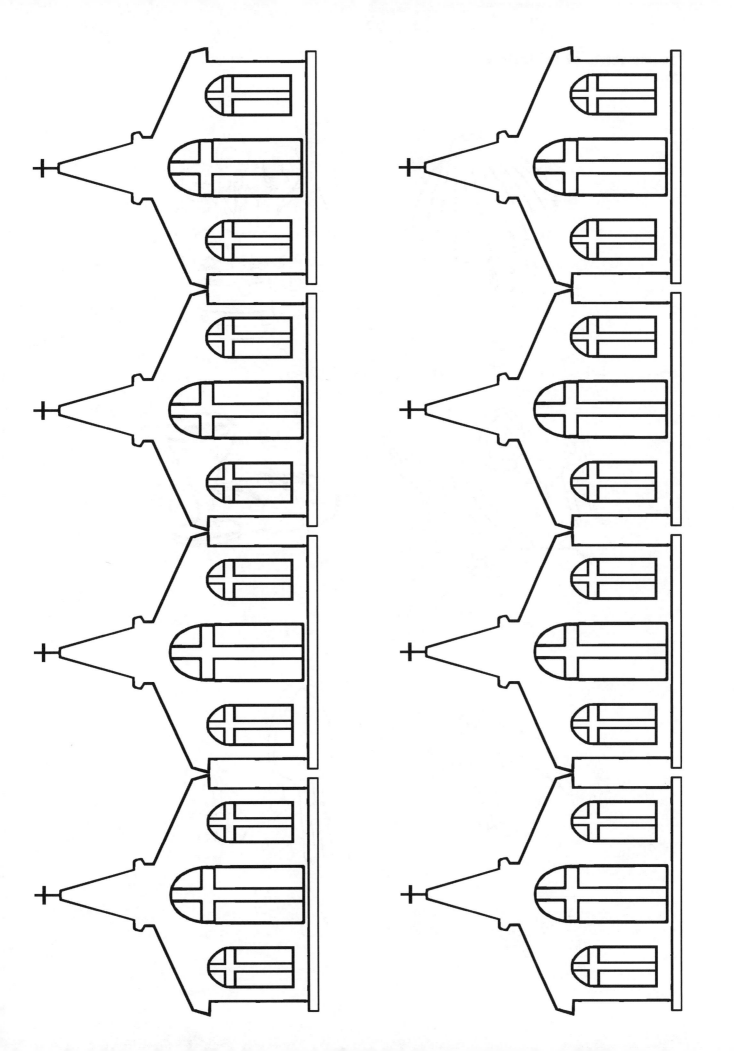

15. THE GOOD SHEPHERD AND THE SACRAMENT OF RECONCILIATION

Objective:

To introduce the children to the concept of reconciliation based on the loving example of Jesus as the Good Shepherd.

Setting:

There is a large open area in the center of the room. One section of the area is "rocky" (large boxes wrapped in brown paper or garbage bags), and another area has a flowing stream (blue tablecloths draped as water, with several green plants near it). On a back wall is a large poster with the words "Poor Choice" and a bridge of the letters "R E C O N C I L I A T I O N" leading from the "Poor Choice" poster to a large red heart. (You may wish to simply use the concept of "Bad Choice" and "Good Choice" or "Poor Choice" and "God's Choice.")

Activity Summary:

The children are involved in a short play on the parable of the lost sheep. Following the skit, the Narrator and the shepherd together tie the concept of "being lost" as the result of poor behavior choices and "being found" through the sacrament of Reconciliation. Then the children, along with their parents, discuss whether pictures in the baskets on their tables (or — if older children are involved — descriptive scenarios) are examples of "bad choices" or "good choices," and they glue them on the appropriate posters. After they finish this activity station, they are free to go to the craft area and make a "shepherd puppet" to remember today's lesson.

Skit Supplies:

- Shepherd cloak and staff (if available)
- Rocks (cardboard box with "scrunched newspaper bunches" — to give an uneven surface — taped on and covered with brown or black paper)
- Stream (blue tablecloth)
- Plants

The Good Shepherd and the Sacrament of Reconciliation

- Large poster saying "Poor Choice"
- Large heart saying "Good Choice" or "God's Choice"
- Letters spelling RECONCILIATION
- Pictures showing good and poor behavior choices (used religious education textbooks are a great and easy source for this)
- Baskets to hold pictures
- Tape or glue

Script:

(As the families arrive, the children are asked to please sit in the cleared space in the center of the room.)

Narrator: Boys and girls, we would like to tell you the story of the Good Shepherd. A long time ago, there was a shepherd who had 100 sheep. He was very proud of his sheep, and loved each one in a very special way. Every day he took the sheep to eat sweet grass and to drink cool water. He kept them safe from wild animals.

(Shepherd walks in and walks around the room, patting different sheep, and saying things like "Your wool looks so white today"; "How is the grass — sweet enough?"; and so on.)

Narrator: One night, the shepherd counted his sheep. *(Shepherd starts pointing and counting with exaggeration.)*

(One previously selected student, already sitting at the side of the group, wanders away, looking curious as to what is happening elsewhere beyond the confines of the meadow they are in now. He peeks in the "bushes," crosses the "stream," slowly meandering around the room.)

(Shepherd, looking very worried, again starts pointing and counting his sheep.)

Narrator: One lamb was lost! The shepherd left the other sheep in a safe place. Then he looked everywhere for the lost sheep! He climbed rocks and pushed through thorny bushes, he crossed streams, and he called and called!

(The Shepherd may wish to huddle the sheep together and pat them on the head, before he begins his search for the lost one. He then gazes around the room, scratches his head, looks in the bushes, crosses the streams, peeks around the rocks, etc.)

Narrator: It was getting dark, and the shepherd was afraid of a wild animal finding the lost sheep before he did!

(The lost sheep looks up in the sky, begins to act afraid, and curls up with his knees to his chest, looking scared as the night approaches.)

Narrator: At last the shepherd found the lost lamb! He was so happy that his little sheep was safe! He hugged the sheep and brought it back to the others.

Shepherd: *Thank goodness I've found you! You are safe now. The other sheep will be happy to have you home with us! Look! I've found him!*

Shepherd (Addressing the children): Boys and girls, the good shepherd is like Jesus. He wants us to know from this story that no matter where we wander away, He will always look for us until He finds us because He loves us so much!

Narrator: Yes, Jesus is a lot like the shepherd. He never wants us to be lost or unhappy. Sometimes, we may do things that we know are wrong, and we walk away from God. Like the shepherd, God wants to take care of us and give us all that we need. When we make poor choices of behavior, we wander off on another path than the one the Good Shepherd has prepared for us. He looks for us everywhere!

If we ask for God's forgiveness when we have done something wrong and wandered away from Him, He is always ready to forgive us. When we ask for God's forgiveness, we call that Reconciliation.

On your tables there are baskets with pictures in them. The pictures show children with their friends and family in their neighborhood and school. Look at what the children are doing and talk with your Mom or Dad, then decide whether the picture shows a Good Choice of behavior, or a Poor Choice of behavior, and glue it on the poster.

Our posters on the wall show us that, even when we have made a "Poor Choice of Behavior," the bridge of Reconciliation brings us back to the Love of Jesus. When you are done, please join us at the craft table.

Good Shepherd Puppets Craft:

Supplies
For each puppet:
- One body (one paint stirring stick, with triangle or rectangle of felt, scrap material, or heavy paper glued to both front and back)
- One head (Styrofoam ball, 3" diameter) *
- Two eyes (craft googly eyes)
- One narrow cloth for arms
- One cloth headcovering
- Two pipecleaners (headband and hook)
- Beard and hair (scraps of yarn or fun fur)

* Attach the heads to the paint sticks ahead of time by inserting one end, with glue, into a slit cut into the ball so that the children have enough time to finish their puppet.

Craft Directions
Glue eyes onto front of head. Glue on hair.
Add beard, if desired.

The Good Shepherd and the Sacrament of Reconciliation

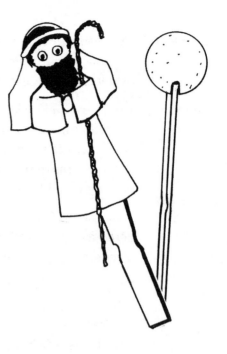

Glue on headcovering and hold in place with a half pipe cleaner wrapped around the crown of the head.

Roll or fold narrow cloth into a strip about 10 to 12 inches long, glue onto center of the back. Also hold arms in position in front with dab of glue.

Bend a whole pipecleaner into a hook.

Wedge or glue hook in arms.

Optional: Add color to face with crayons.

Refreshments:

Large pretzel rods

Powdered sugar donut holes

Sign on refreshment table:

Pretzel rods help us remember the Good Shepherd's staff.

White donut holes remind us of sheep!

Project Checklist

_____

_____

_____

_____

_____

_____

_____

_____

_____

_____

16. LITURGICAL YEAR

Objective:

To offer families an opportunity to learn "hands-on" about the liturgical year, and to provide take-home crafts as references to help them understand, communicate, and pray together focusing on the seasonal worship cycle of our faith.

Activity Summary:

The families are welcomed and introduced to the topic by a brief introduction using a "family calendar" compared to a liturgical calendar. Then they are invited to visit various displays around the room of lectionaries/sacramentaries; priest's vestments and stoles of the various seasons; and some of the actual symbols used — such as the pitcher and bowl used for washing of the feet on Holy Thursday, Paschal Candle, Advent Wreath, chalice and paten, various sanctuary banners, etc. Catechists are available to answer questions if needed. There is a "Cycles of the Liturgical Year" craft that the children color in the seasons; and all families receive an "In God's Time … at Home" book to take home with discussion questions to use throughout the six seasons. (If desired, this "In God's Time … at Home" book may be assembled by the families picking up the appropriate pages at each of the seasonal tables and hole punching the top to put through a paper fastener or simply stapling the set.)

Activity Setting:

Tables are set with the items listed earlier, and an additional table prepared for the "Cycles of the Liturgical Year" craft. The refreshment area with a variety of foods to represent the seasons — as much as possible (Christmas cookies, pretzels, fruit, etc.) — is covered until after the families have visited the display areas.

Display Items:

- Priest vestments and stoles for all the seasons
- Lectionary and Children's Lectionary, if available
- Sacramentary
- Paten and chalice
- Book of Gospels
- Altar linens
- Water cruet and bowl
- Liturgical oils
- Holy Water

Liturgical Year

- Basin and pitcher used for Holy Thursday
- Paschal Candle
- Advent Wreath
- Various sanctuary banners

Script:

Welcome to our Family Gathering on our liturgical year! That may sound like a hard word to say and understand, but it means simply our calendar of Sundays. Just like we all have calendars like this *(hold up a calendar)* in our homes that help us know what we have to do, even how we plan activities for winter or summer happenings — our Church has a calendar that begins four weeks before Christmas each year. The readings you hear every week in Church are repeated every three years. They are all found in this book, called the Lectionary. These three years are called Year A, Year B, and — what else do you think? — Year C. When you have time, we have several of these books out for you to look through. Years ago, Bible scholars chose these readings for us to gain the most wisdom for each particular time of the Church year. Like for the weeks coming up to Christmas, we have certain readings, and for Easter and Lent we have specific readings to help us with our faith. Besides the certain readings, we have special colors that are on banners in Church, or on the robes the priest wears. We have many symbols also. Symbols for Advent — the four weeks before Christmas; for Christmas; for Ordinary Time; for Lent, for the special three days before Easter — Holy Thursday, Good Friday, and Easter Sunday; and for Easter itself. How many days are there of Easter? You may think just one day — but it is actually a season of 50 days, beginning on Easter Sunday and ending on Pentecost Sunday, which celebrates the gift of the Holy Spirit. To help you remember all of these things, we have set up around the room displays of different items and colors we use in worship in our six seasons of the Church year. Some may be very familiar to you — like the vestments the priest wears — and some might not be. What month does our family calendar begin with? January, right? Our Church year begins four weeks before Christmas — we call that "Advent." The other seasons are: Christmas; Ordinary Time; Lent; the Triduum — the word means the three holy days before Easter — Holy Thursday, Good Friday, and Easter Sunday; and Ordinary Time again. Ordinary Time includes the Sundays in the Church year not directly related to Christmas and Easter. After you have visited the displays, we invite you to make a simple craft to take home to help you remember the different colors used for the different seasons. *(Hold up craft and show where they are to color the spaces for each season.)*

Our liturgical year helps us grow stronger in our faith. Just like at home, each of us changes from one season to the next and from one calendar year to the next. With our liturgical calendar, we are brought closer to God as we hear the Bible passages and use the same symbols each year to help us remember how much God loves us in every season! Before you leave today, please take one of these *(hold up "In God's Time … At Home")* with you for your family to use throughout the Church seasons.

Crafts Supplies and Directions:

"Cycles of the Liturgical Year" Craft

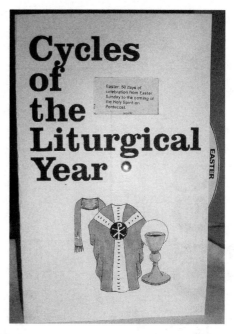

Craft Supplies

- Templates of the liturgical year cycle — two sheets
- Red, white, purple, and green crayons
- Paper fasteners

Craft Directions

Cut out window on the cover sheet.

Fold the outside sheet.

Color in the space below each description of the liturgical cycle as indicated.

Poke through the two sheets with a paper fastener.

"In God's Time ... at Home" booklet

Craft Supplies

- Booklet pages (see pages 148–157) cut apart on dotted lines
- Hole punch and paper fasteners or stapler

Craft Directions

[Booklet may be assembled beforehand or by the parents at the gathering.]

Cut booklet pages apart on the dotted lines. Assemble in order. Fasten together by chosen method.

Refreshments:

A variety of pretzels or hot cross buns

Christmas cookies (cut out in angel shapes, etc.)

Variety of fruit

Beverages

Cycles
of
the
Liturgical
Year

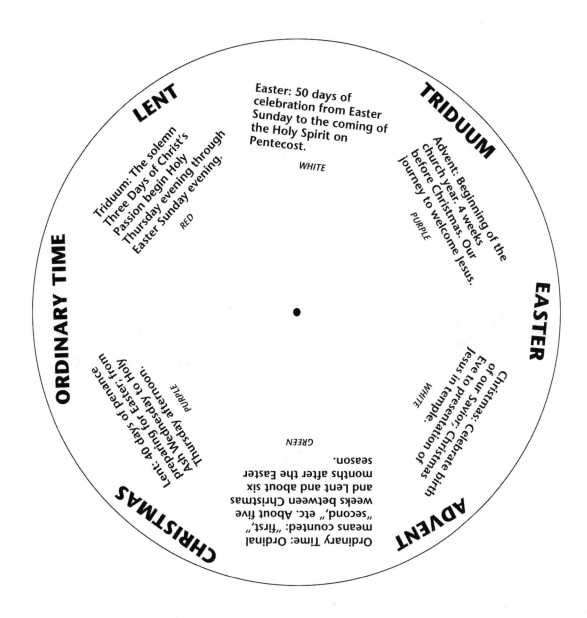

LENT

TRIDUUM

ORDINARY TIME

EASTER

CHRISTMAS

ADVENT

Easter: 50 days of celebration from Easter Sunday to the coming of the Holy Spirit on Pentecost.

WHITE

Triduum: The solemn Three Days of Christ's Passion begin Holy Thursday evening through Easter Sunday evening.

RED

Advent: Beginning of the church year. 4 weeks before Christmas. Our journey to welcome Jesus.

PURPLE

Christmas: Celebrate birth of our Savior; Christmas Eve to presentation of Jesus in temple.

WHITE

Lent: 40 days of penance preparing for Easter; from Ash Wednesday to Holy Thursday afternoon.

PURPLE

Ordinary Time: Ordinal means counted: "first," "second," etc. About five weeks between Christmas and Lent and about six months after the Easter season.

GREEN

"God's Time . . . At Home"

Advent is a time of preparing — of looking into our hearts to see how we can be more loving and giving to our family and friends.

What did you see in your heart today?

Advent

Advent is a time of reaching out to other people who may be feeling lonely or sad.

To whom have you reached out today?

Advent is a time of not just waiting for Christmas morning gifts — but of actively preparing ourselves to welcome Jesus.

We prepare ourselvs by spending time with Jesus in prayer. Not only talking, but quietly listening to what He says to us.

What did you hear today?

Advent is a time of great joy!

Who have you hugged today?

Christmas

Talk about the baptisms of family members and sign each other with water in the Sign of the Cross saying:

I — BELONG — TO — GOD

Mary, Joseph, and Jesus trusted God the Father in all things.

Share as a family a time when God answered a prayer.

Ordinary Time

The Magi brought baby Jesus gifts.

What special gifts or talents do you have?

How did you give them to Jesus today?

What helps you to know that someone is a follower of Jesus?

When have you stopped yourself from gossiping — knowing it was wrong.

Jesus healed many people of physical and mental diseases.

How have you helped take away someone's pain today?

Share a time when a friend helped you, and how it felt to have someone care.

At times the disciples didn't understand Jesus and questioned Him.

What question would you ask Jesus?

Snack on unsalted popcorn or pretzels, then the salted variety.

Read and talk about Matthew 5:13.

What type of "light" are you to the world?

. . . a "Beacon" that others follow?

. . . a "Lighthouse" that brings others to safety?

. . . a "Candle — warm and inviting?

Discuss as a family other types of light in terms of faith in Jesus.

Lent

Once, Peter was afraid to say he was a follower of Jesus.

When has it been hard for you to follow Jesus?

Lent is a season to fast (eating more simple food); to pray and listen to God; and to give to those in need.

Discuss how you can do this as a family.

Hold ice cubes tightly until your hands become numb, then wrap them in a heated towel. God's love is like this. Sometimes we get "numb" to the sins we do, and God's love takes the cold away and covers us with warmth and protection.

What are you tempted to do that you know is wrong?

The disciples slept when Jesus needed them.

When have you disappointed someone you love?

As a family, watch a video of the events of Holy Week and the resurrected Jesus.

With whom do you identify?

One disciple, Thomas, doubted Jesus had risen. What do you believe that you cannot see?

(Electricity, sound waves, what else?)

Easter

After the resurrection, Jesus came to His disciples and said, "Peace be with you."

What *place* means peace to you?

How do you picture "peace?"

Bake marshmallows in a "crescent roll" — when you open them, the marshmallow has disappeared. Like the empty tomb — what was there is gone!

What changes can you make today to follow Jesus more closely?

Read Acts 2:1–4 and act it out with a fan blowing and "tongues of fire" (tape orange and yellow flames on a red paper hat); then babble in "different languages!"

Early Christians used the sign of a fish to meet secretly and pray.

What would be your family's "secret sign?"

Talk about different items in your home and how they are similar to the Holy Spirit.

. . . A flashlight shows the way.

. . . Tools repair and build things.

. . . Hot pads protect you from harm.

Use your imagination!

Ordinary Time

Bake bread together, thinking about how each ingredient can symbolize our Christian faith.

How do you picture heaven?

Pray as a family for those people who feel alone and uncared for by others.

Listen to what God asks you to do for them.

ORDINARY TIME— 2

What are you afraid of?

ORDINARY TIME —

Look up some of these words in a dictionary and talk about how they relate to Jesus and His disciples (us):

meek, gentle, humble, burdened, and yoke.

ORDINARY TIME — 3

Read Luke 12:27–29.

What do you worry about God providing for you?

ORDINARY TIME —

Read together the Parable of the Sower (Matthew 13:3–9). What are some of the 'birds,' 'thorns,' 'scorching sun,' and 'shallow soil' that stop our faith from growing?

ORDINARY TIME — 4

Jesus talked a lot about finding things that were lost.

When have you lost something and were overjoyed when you found it again?

ORDINARY TIME —

Jesus said, "Go out and make disciples of all men."

Is there one person you know who needs to hear about Jesus today?

ORDINARY TIME — 8

Jesus asked His disciples, "Who do you say I am?"

What words describe Jesus to you?

ORDINARY TIME —11

Fill in with your own "Be-Attitude' . . .

Blessed are you when _____ , for you will _____ .

ORDINARY TIME — 9

Look at a mustard seed and read Mark 5:30

ORDINARY TIME — 12

Open an apple and see how generous God is!

1 apple = 30 seeds = 30 apple trees = thousands of apples = hundred thousand trees, etc.

GOD GENEROUSLY PROVIDES
FOR OUR NEEDS!

ORDINARY TIME — 10

Jesus said, "Love your neighbor as yourself."

Who is your neighbor in need of love?

ORDINARY TIME — 13

Read Mark 10:13

Children are precious to Jesus.

Plan as a family how to reach out to children who are in need. . .

. . . in your community

. . . in the world

ORDINARY TIME — 14

Jesus said, "Love your enemies — do good to those who hate you."

Who — for you — is hard to love?

ORDINARY TIME —

Jesus said, "Be alert! The hour is coming — be watchful!"

What are you waiting for?

ORDINARY TIME— 15

Shepherds are mentioned a lot in Scripture.

Learn about the life of a shepherd this week.

What does it teach you about Jesus?

ORDINARY TIME —

Look at a triangle or a shamrock and discuss how it relates to the Trinity — three in one. Is there another image of the Trinity that you can think of?

ORDINARY TIME — 16

When did you last forgive someone?

How did it feel?

ORDINARY TIME — 1

When were you last forgiven by someone for something you said or did that was hurtful?

How did it feel?

Read Luke 11:1–4.

Pray the Lord's Prayer thanking Jesus for this gift!

What word describes Jesus best?

Good Shepherd?

Best Friend?

Teacher?

Savior?

Why?

This week, take a quiet moment and make the Sign of the Cross on each other's foreheads, while saying this blessing:

"God has claimed you in love to be His child. Trust in Him always."

What does Jesus look like?

What is your favorite story about Jesus?

Project Checklist

17. GOD MAKES A BEAUTIFUL WORLD

Objective:

This Family Gathering is designed to be very simple in presentation and preparation (perfect for a summer family get-together after Mass or Church services).

Activity Summary:

Families work together with a script and a prepared envelope of pictures to re-create day by day the origin of the world and all its creatures. This activity is followed by a community building "yarn toss" where everyone present reflects on their "favorite part" of the created world. At the end of the activity, all enjoy making "Creation Cups" at the refreshment table.

Setting:

Guests are handed a large envelope as they enter. Tables and chairs with centerpieces of brown circles cut from construction paper (or brown commercial paper towels) topped with crushed chocolate wafer cookies and gummy worms and bugs. Refreshment table is off to the side and covered.

Script:

God Creates A Beautiful World

Long ago, God made the world out of nothing. But it didn't look the way it does now. There were no people, animals, birds, trees or flowers! Everything was lonely and dark. *(Find the black papers and glue them on your world.)*

So God made the light. He gave the light the name Day. He called the darkness Night. This was the first day of creation. *(Find the "Light" and put it on your world …)*

On the second day of creation, God made the sky. He named the sky Heaven. And on the third day, God made the oceans and lakes and the dry land. Then He made the grass grow and covered the land with all kinds of flowers, bushes, and trees. *(Have fun by finding the sky, water, and the flowers and tree pictures, and paste them on your world.)*

The fourth day of creation, God put the sun, moon, and stars in the sky! *(Did you find the sun and the stars to paste on your world?)*

On the fifth day, God made all the wonderful fish in the sea, big and small. He made all the birds too — ducks and geese that could swim, eagles and robins to live in the woods and fields. *(It's time to paste the fish and the birds on the world.)*

Then, on the sixth day, He made the animals — rabbits, elephants, and even bees and butterflies. He made so many different varieties! *(Now, paste your favorite animals and things that crawl upon the ground or fly in the air on your world.)*

And God was very pleased with all that He had made! The world was beautiful! The seventh day, God rested.

Boys and girls, turn over the world you just created. See the face of Jesus. All of creation — each star, each flower, each snake, each animal, each of us, is part of God's plan — and Jesus ties all of us together in His Love. We are all "connected!" To help us understand our "connectedness," we have a ball of yarn to toss to each other. When you catch the yarn, wrap it around your wrist, and tell everyone what is your favorite part of God's created world — is it an animal you love the most, is it the ocean, the stars, the flowers in the garden, or is it the sun on a warm spring day? When everyone has had a chance to share with the yarn, we have scissors on the table for you to cut off your part of the yarn and use it to make a mobile of your created world to hang in your room!

Supplies:

- Large envelopes with an Earth template punched at the top to be hung as a mobile, each containing (option — find magazine pictures of all these items):
- Picture of Jesus on the reverse side of the Earth template
- Black pieces of paper (about 5" x 7")
- Yellow pieces of construction paper that say, "Let there be light!" (about 5" x 7")
- Star stickers, yellow suns (construction paper), white moon
- Sky, earth, mountains, water (oceans/lakes), trees, flowers, plants, animals, birds, reptiles, etc.
- People of various nationalities
- A ball of yarn
- Scissors
- Glue and glue applicators

Refreshments:

"Creation Cups"

Have the refreshment table prepared with the following items:

Clear plastic cups
Chocolate pudding — night
Vanilla pudding — day
Blue frosting decorating gel — sky and water
Butterscotch and chocolate chips — mountains
Shredded coconut, tinted green — grass
Yellow sprinkles for the stars, or if available, cake decorating edible stars — stars
Gummy worms
Animal and people cookies/crackers
Beverages

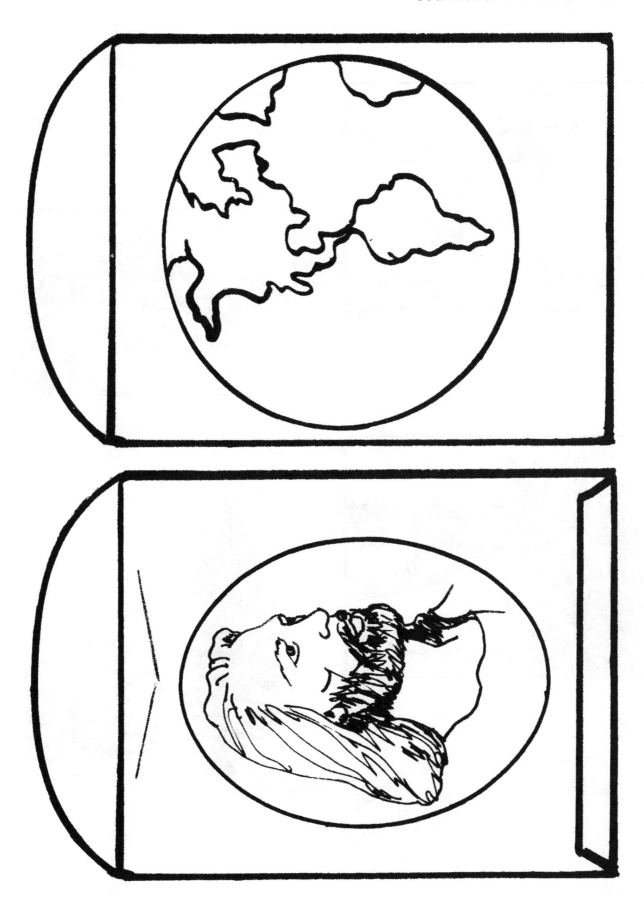

18. THE SEVEN DAYS OF CREATION

Objective:

To help the families connect with the awesomeness of God's creative spirit!

Activity Summary:

The children, with their parent's assistance, create a mobile (as illustrated) of the seven days of creation. Each of the seven parts of the mobile has a Scripture verse label to attach.

Activity Setting:

There are seven areas set up with all the craft supplies needed for each "day." There is an additional table set up with yarn and hole punches to complete the project. The refreshment and hospitality area is in another part of the room.

Script:

We want to welcome everyone to our Family Gathering on the Seven Days of Creation. Today we are making a mobile to hang in your home to help us remember how God our Father is a loving Creator. Each of us and all of nature — every tree, animal, flower, mountain, everything — was designed by God and is loved by God! Let us listen now to the words of Scripture:

(A person with a commanding voice and presence reads *Genesis 1:1-31.* Or if there are very young children who would become restless with the length of this reading, it would be also effective to continue with this passage alone):

"God looked at everything He had made, and He found it very good."

We know that God loves all He creates. And remember that each of us is one of His special creations.

Now, we invite you to go to all of the seven tables. You do not need to go in any special order of days. After you finish each of the seven parts, please come to the back table where we have hole punches and yarn to put the mobile together.

The Seven Days of Creation

Craft Supplies and Instructions:

Creation Mobile

Supplies

(Listed by day of creation with instructions)

- Glue
- Staplers
- Hole punches
- Yarn
- Verses (provided see page 168) copied and cut out at each of the "seven days stations"

Directions

First Day (Meat tray, black construction paper — cut to fit size of meat tray)
Glue black paper and verse to one side.

Second Day (Dessert-size paper plate, blue shiny paper on "water" side, plain blue paper for "sky" side, goldfish crackers, cotton balls)
Glue verse and clouds on the "sky" side. Glue fish on the "water" side.

Third Day (Sandpaper squares, heavy blue paper on reverse side, colored sand, markers or crayons, tissue paper scraps)
Glue verse onto the blue "water" side. On the sandpaper side, draw grass, plants, trees with glue, then sprinkle with colored sand. Or glue on tissue paper flowers.

Fourth Day (Small plastic lid, black paper circle on one side, yellow circle on reverse, craft foam/stickers of suns, moons, and stars)
Glue verse onto the side with yellow, "sunny" paper.
Glue moon and stars onto side with black paper.

Fifth Day (Small cardboard roll, cut construction paper — red for cardinals, blue for blue birds, brown for wrens, etc. to cover roll — googly eyes, yellow paper beaks, and wings/feathers)
Glue construction paper on "bird."
Glue verse on or inside the roll. Glue wings/feathers, paper beak, and "googly eyes" on the bird.

Sixth Day (Animal face paper plate, CD, small Jesus sticker)
Glue verse onto the animal face, and decorate it, if you wish. Glue CD on reverse side and place Jesus sticker in center.

Seventh Day (Cardboard rectangle, yellow semicircles, fabric rectangles for blanket, smaller swatches for pillow, cotton stuffing)
Make a pillow and blanket with the material, stuff with a little cotton, and staple onto the cardboard (or have a helper staple for young children).

Tuck the foam circle under the blanket and staple or glue it on the pillow. Staple verse to bottom end of bed.

Punch holes in each "day" and string together with yarn.

Refreshments:

Dirt Pudding Cups (chocolate pudding with gummy worms peeking out of crushed cookie topping)

Trail Mix (made of Teddy Grahams, animal and people crackers, gummy bears and worms, goldfish crackers, candy corn, etc.) in baggie with label, "Taste the Goodness of Creation!"

THE FIRST DAY: God said, "Let there be light," and there was light. God saw how good the light was, and separated the light from the darkness. God called the light "day," and the darkness He called "night."

THE SECOND DAY: God made an opening in the "waters." He pushed the waters away and made a space He called the "Heavens."

THE THIRD DAY: On the third day God separated the waters from the dry land. He called the dry land "earth" and filled the dry land with all living plants and trees.

THE FOURTH DAY: God made the stars and the two great lights which light up the heavens. The Sun gave light during the day, and the Moon gave light during the night.

THE FIFTH DAY: God created all the animals that live in the sea, and the birds that live in the sky.

THE SIXTH DAY: God created all the animals that live on the earth. But the animals were not enough. God created Man and Woman to share His Life and His Love.

ON THE SEVENTH DAY: God saw that all He had made was very good. Then, He rested.

THE FIRST DAY: God said, "Let there be light," and there was light. God saw how good the light was, and separated the light from the darkness. God called the light "day," and the darkness He called "night."

THE SECOND DAY: God made an opening in the "waters." He pushed the waters away and made a space He called the "Heavens."

THE THIRD DAY: On the third day God separated the waters from the dry land. He called the dry land "earth" and filled the dry land with all living plants and trees.

THE FOURTH DAY: God made the stars and the two great lights which light up the heavens. The Sun gave light during the day, and the Moon gave light during the night.

THE FIFTH DAY: God created all the animals that live in the sea, and the birds that live in the sky.

THE SIXTH DAY: God created all the animals that live on the earth. But the animals were not enough. God created Man and Woman to share His Life and His Love.

ON THE SEVENTH DAY: God saw that all He had made was very good. Then, He rested.

19. NOAH BUILT AN ARK!

Objective:

To familiarize children with the biblical story of Noah; by involving them in acting out the Scripture passage and making crafts to remind them of the lesson.

Setting:

A room large enough to accommodate the expected number of children in a center empty space. A cardboard ark has been assembled and is in another part of the room. The snack table is off to the side and is "covered" to indicate the activity will take place first before the hospitality begins. Two or three tables have been prepared for the crafts.

Activity Summary:

The children participate in an impromptu skit with one adult actor as "God," followed by the making of three crafts and enjoying a theme-related snack (a variety of rainbow-colored jello in clear plastic cups).

Activity and Play:

Helpers are at the entrance to the room, with "Animal Signs" to place around the necks of the children as they come in. These animal signs are pictures of individual animals taped or printed on 8.5" x 11" paper that have been hole-punched and yarn attached at the ends for the children to wear around their neck. (Young children who are not yet readers can identify the animal and, when asked by "Noah," will find their partner.) The helpers make sure each "animal" has a partner, as they greet and place the "sign" with the yarn loop on each child.

Dependent on the expected number of children, there are "Noah" and "Noah's Family" signs also, for boys and girls who are middle elementary ages.

Neck sign

Actors Needed:

God
Older children or teens as helpers

Noah Built an Ark!

Play Supply List:

- Animal pictures (two of each kind) on 8.5" x 11" papers, with a yarn loop attached by hole punch/or tape
- "Noah" picture and "Noah's Family" pictures on 1-5 (depends on the expected number of children) prepared the same way
- Large pieces of cardboard, taped together and cut as an "ark" (black marker lines help to define it as a boat — ark can rest against several folding chairs to keep upright)
- Numbers 1 through 40 on individual sheets of paper, written large enough so all can see
- Water squirt bottles
- A "bird" prop — or the two children designated as the "dove duo"
- A sprig of greenery
- "Sun" hat (see Family Gathering 8) and yellow drape or tablecloth
- Rainbow banner
- Someone to play "God" with a loud booming voice and presence
- Older children or parents to assist

Script:

(After all the children have an animal or Noah sign …)
(GOD comes into the room.)

GOD   (In a booming yet gentle voice): NOAH! NOAH!

NOAH: YES? (All the Noahs come forward.)

GOD   (Gathers all the Noahs around him.)

GOD: Noah — I have some very important news for you! You must build a boat — a strong boat that will keep your family safe for many days. I'll tell you just how to do it.

(Picking up the ark pieces, God and the Noahs assemble the ark. God goes around commenting "Good Job" "Well done!" scratching his chin as if he is checking out the Noahs' building efforts; patting the Noahs on their backs, etc. Once the ark is up, GOD says:)

GOD: Great, Noah! It is done — you and your family will be safe now for a long time. It is going to rain, Noah — RAIN! RAIN! RAIN! There will be so much RAIN that the Earth is going to flood — that is why I had you build this boat! You have always been very faithful and prayed. You are a good man, and that is why I saved you from the flood. We must do one more thing before the rains begin. I need you to bring one mother and one father of every animal in the world onto the boat with you. Now hurry, Noah, and gather the animals in by pairs.

(The "animal" children find their match — with the help of the Noahs and Noah's Family — and go into [behind] the boat.)

(GOD looks around to make sure all the animals are safely on board.)

GOD: NOAH! ARE YOU READY?

NOAHS: YES!

GOD: The rain begins! *(If possible, older children or teens hold up large numbers on signs numbered 1 through 40 and run around the room — other helpers are squirting water on the ark with spray bottles.) GOD stands to the side.*

Then the "rain" stops.

GOD comes out from the side — and calls in a loud voice — "NOAH!"
NOAH: Yes?
GOD: Noah, the sun is coming out! The rains have stopped!

(The "SUN" peeks out from the side hallway and then gallops across the room.) (The "Sun" wears a plastic yellow construction hat that had been slit at the top to fit in yellow foam board rays [see Family Gathering 8] and a draped yellow plastic tablecloth worn like a poncho.)

GOD: Noah, send a dove out to fly! If it returns to you with a green leaf — then you know there is dry land again!

The Dove *(child wearing that sign)* leaves the ark and goes into another room and returns with a green leaf.

GOD: Noah, as a promise to you that I will never flood the earth again, I give you this rainbow. Whenever it rains, remember My promise to you and look for the rainbow!

(Older children or teen helpers unfurl a rainbow banner.)

Crafts:

Three areas of crafts are set up for the children.
1. An ark
2. Animal masks
3. Rainbow disk

Crafts Supplies and Instructions:

Ark
- Sandpaper cut into "ark" shapes
- Small pieces of brown, black, and tan construction or computer paper to "build" the ark
- Glue and either Q-tips or craft sticks to apply the glue

Animal Masks
- Lunch bags with a variety of items to create the animal faces
- Googly eyes, scissors, pipe cleaners, paper scraps, glue, markers, cotton balls, etc.
- Several prepared examples

Animal mask

Rainbow Craft
- Color rainbow template (provided)
- Glue onto a CD

Noah Built an Ark!

Refreshments:

Jello in a variety of colors (red, orange, yellow, blue, and green) in clear plastic individual cups (the 8-ounce kind) prepared ahead of time and placed in a rainbow shape on the refreshment table. As many prefer a whipped topping, some is available also, as are baskets of multicolored cookies or other snacks.

Coffee and juice or lemonade

(This is a great time to use up the "odds and ends" of different colored napkins and plastic tablecloths!)

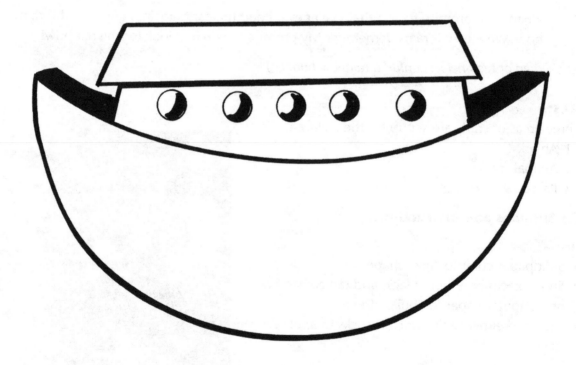

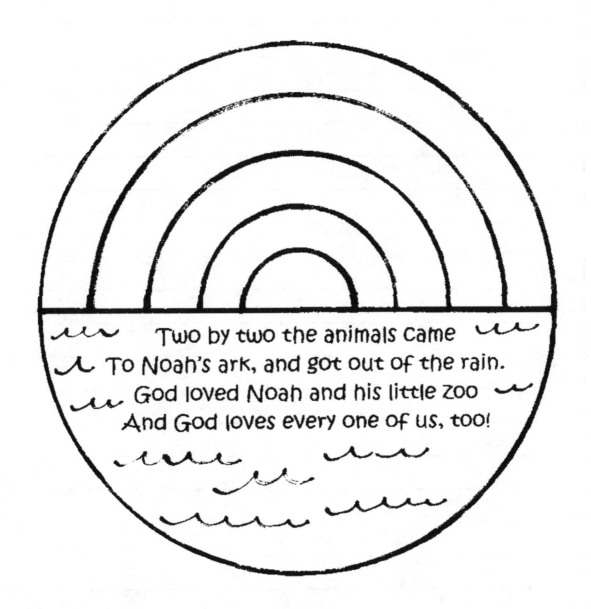

Two by two the animals came
To Noah's ark, and got out of the rain.
God loved Noah and his little zoo
And God loves every one of us, too!

Project Checklist

_____

_____

_____

_____

_____

_____

_____

_____

_____

_____

_____

_____

_____

_____

_____

_____

_____

20. MOSES AND THE JOURNEY TO FREEDOM

Objective:
To familiarize the children with the story of Moses as presented in Exodus.

Setting:
The families arrive and are asked to sit at tables arranged in a long line facing the wall. On the wall is a long banner depicting very large coloring book outlines of the following items: A basket with green ferns and milk pods surrounding it, a kneeling "princess," a "princely" man, outline of a brick wall, a shepherd and sheep, branches of a bush, sandals, a large heart, a barbell and a staff, a large heart with a crown and the word "Closed!" on it, a large black piece of paper covering a portion of the banner, a sea with the two sides of the water raised up, exposing a path, and a large mountain.

Activity Summary:
The story of Moses is read (script follows) while the children come forward with items from trays on their tables to "fill in" the coloring book sketches. After this activity, the children may make Ten Commandment Tablets and share a snack of "Plague Cupcakes."

Script:
Today we are going to tell the story of Moses, who was called by God to lead the Jewish people out of slavery in Egypt to freedom. The items on your tables will be part of our story. Also, our refreshments are part of the story of Moses, and we will share them after we finish our project.

The Jewish people had been slaves for many, many years. One Egyptian king became worried that there were too many Jewish people — he made a law that all Jewish baby boys had to be killed.

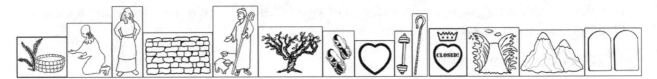

Moses Journey wall art

Moses and the Journey to Freedom

One mother, trusting in God to take care of her baby, placed her baby boy carefully in a basket and put the basket among reeds at the river's shore. To fill in our picture on the wall, we need to make the basket, the reeds, and the sea. (The children select the appropriate items and come to the wall banner to glue/tape them on. Adults are available to assist. With each figure outline of the banner, this pattern will continue as the Narrator pauses for the children to select the items and come forward to place them on the banner.)

Then, an Egyptian princess found the basket and took the baby boy home to raise as her own child, and she named the baby "Moses."

Let's fill in the princess's dress — with bright green cloth and gold trim.

Moses grew to be a handsome man, almost like a prince himself. Let us dress him in his fancy clothes — pretty blue cloth and gold trim. One day, Moses saw how hard the Jewish slaves worked making bricks — and he became very angry. He left Egypt to become a shepherd.

Let us now make a shepherd and the sheep. Be sure to look for a sheep's eye and his pink nose too!

After many years, when Moses was an old man, he was tending his sheep — like he did every day, when all of a sudden — he saw a bush that was on fire — but was not being destroyed! Then God's voice spoke loudly, "MOSES! MOSES! TAKE OFF YOUR SANDALS! YOU ARE STANDING ON HOLY GROUND! So, Moses took off his sandals and stood before the burning bush.

Boys and girls, let's fill in our burning bush and place the sandals next to it.

God told Moses that he had a special purpose. God wanted Moses to go back to Egypt and lead the Jewish people to freedom! God gave Moses power, strength, and a loving heart to make the journey.

Let's fill in our symbols of the staff, the barbell, and the loving heart.

Moses went back to Egypt and told the Pharaoh (the king of Egypt) that God wanted the Jewish slaves to be free. The Pharaoh had a very hard heart, a heart of stone, and he refused to set the Jewish people free.

Let us now put "rocks" on the King's heart that was closed to the requests of Moses.

God sent many plagues to Egypt to try to change the King's mind. God sent frogs, bugs, darkness, lightning, and many other things to frighten the king and make him change his mind.

On your tables are stickers of bugs, snakes, and other things to represent the plagues sent to the Egyptian king.

Finally, the King had had enough and told Moses to take the Jewish people out of Egypt and lead them through the sea to new freedom. God made the sea part in two — and provided a lifesaving path right down the middle.

(Children will place lifesavers on the path.)

After Moses and the Jews were free, the Pharaoh changed his mind, and began to chase the Jews across the sea. God then caused the water of the sea to crash down upon the Egyptian army and they were lost in the water.

Let's now make our crashing waves.

Moses then led his people for many years throughout the desert until they came to a mountain. God spoke to Moses again, and gave him the Ten Commandments.

I think we have someone who wants to tell us about the Ten Commandments.

(As the Narrator concludes the script, "God" comes out of a hidden area with the following message):

(He holds a cardboard Ten Commandments — covered with "marble" contact paper — and says):

Hello, boys and girls. Yes this is God talking to you again. We have just heard the story of a very good and holy man named Moses. He led My people to freedom over a long journey through the desert. You know, all of us — your Moms and Dads and each of you — are also on a "journey" like Moses. You are on a path to know and love Me more and more each day. I gave Moses the Ten Commandments to help people make right decisions. My rules are to keep you safe and happy. These rules are for you, too. Remember the story of Moses — and remember that I am asking you to follow these rules every day of your life.

Now boys and girls, I have a busy schedule to keep — and must go on my way — but in my wisdom I gave you all very good Moms and Dads to teach you right from wrong. Have them tell you about my Ten Commandments. Good-bye and remember to say your prayers every day.

Activity Supplies:

On the tables where the families are seated are the following items:

- Black and brown scraps of paper, raffia, or hay
- Tops of the "milk pods" (black ovals of foam board, or paper, etc.)
- Blue shiny strips of paper in "wave" shapes to place under the basket
- Bright pieces of fabric, gold ribbon, or cloth to fill in the princess's dress
- Additional pieces of another color of fabric and gold ribbon/cloth to fill in the "princely" figure
- Bricks of painted cardboard or construction paper (or, if available, spray-painted Styrofoam meat trays)
- Tissue paper of red, yellow, and orange twisted/squeezed together to represent the flaming bush
- Sandals — simple open-toe flip-flop sketch in brown or black
- Black or brown pipe cleaners to fill in the staff outline
- Small red felt hearts to fill in the heart of Moses
- Aluminum foil pieces to fill in the "barbell" to represent the strength God gave to Moses
- Black or gray "scrunched" construction paper to glue on the Pharaoh's closed heart to represent rocks
- Gold pieces of ribbon to fill in his crown

- Stickers of snakes, bugs, etc. to place on the black piece of the banner to represent the plagues
- Lifesavers for the journey to freedom across the Red Sea
- Strips of colored shiny paper stapled together to represent the crashing of the water on the Pharaoh's army
- Additional shiny blue water strips to fill in the sea
- Large pieces of brown construction paper to glue on the mountain
- Pieces of rougher, duller cloth to fill in the shepherd; rolled balls of black tissue paper to place on the shepherd's beard
- Pieces of lamb's wool, a pink pom-pom (nose) and a large eye for the sheep

Ten Commandment Tablet Craft:

The children are invited to make their own Ten Commandments. Individual card stock tablets covered in marble-patterned paper are given to the children along with the list of the Ten Commandments, written in simple language.

Supplies
- Card stock cut tablets covered with marble patterned paper
- Sheet of Ten Commandments
- Scissors
- Glue and glue applicators

Craft Introduction
God gave these commandments to help you. What happens when you don't obey these commandments? Who can help you obey them? Think these questions over.

See if you and your parents can come up with the answers. Cut out the printed commandments and glue them onto your "stone tablet."

[See the next page for the commandments.]

Refreshments:

All are invited to share in the refreshments of "Plague Cupcakes." On the hospitality table, trays of frosted cupcakes are placed with the following items:

Gummy snakes or green gumdrops to represent frogs

Chocolate sprinkles to represent the gnats

Red frosting decorating gel for blood

Yellow sprinkles for lightning (cut out models of lightning will help with this)

Beverages

1. Do not worship any God but Me.

Love God more than anything or anyone else.

2. You must not use the name of the Lord your God in vain.

God's name is holy. We use it only in prayer.

3. Remember to observe the Sabbath as a holy day.

God rested on the seventh day of Creation.
Sunday is to be a day when we rest and thank God for all His wonderful gifts to us.

4. Honor your father and your mother.

As children, we obey God and our parents.

5. You must not kill.

ALL life is precious to God.

6. You must not commit adultery.

In God's plan a husband and a wife remain faithful to each other.

7. You must not steal.

God asks us to respects others' belongings.

8. You must not tell lies.

Always tell the truth.

9. You must not envy your neighbor's wife.

God wants us to keep the promises we make.

10. You must not envy your neighbor's goods.

God knows us and gives us what we need.

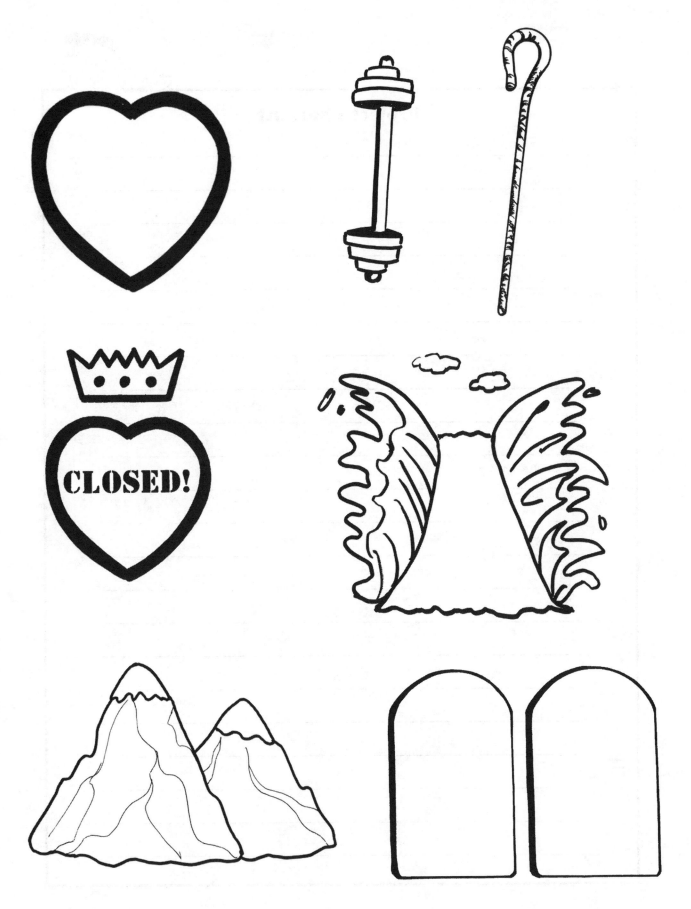

Project Checklist

_____

_____

_____

_____

_____

_____

_____

_____

_____

_____

_____

_____

_____

_____

_____

_____

_____

21. ALL SAINTS

Theme:

Celebrate the lives of the Saints!

Objective:

To emphasize the lessons we learn from the lives of some familiar saints and to offer an alternative holiday celebration that puts the season in a positive focus.

Setting:

Tables and chairs are facing a wall to which a time line is attached. Each table holds at least one symbol of a saint and a supply of booklets and stickers. In front of each date on the time line is a stool, chair, or table to hold the objects that symbolize the saints.

A fishpond: A blue bedsheet hung at a height of about 48 inches.

A craft table supplied with mask-making materials.

Activity Summary:

A Narrator reads a few facts about the saints, and the children bring items representing them from their tables and place them in front of the time line. They also match stickers to the saint's page in the provided booklet (see templates on pages 187-191). Then the children are invited to fish for a prize in the fishpond and to make a mask that shows a good quality about themselves.

Script:

The COMMUNION of SAINTS involves all of us — we are all together, these wonderful people who lived so long ago, and each of us today — we are all connected. We are one family in our love for Jesus. Each of us can be a saint if we put God first in our life.

There have been people of GREAT FAITH who *served* people, *taught* people, *loved* children, *shared* their riches, and *healed* people, all because of their love for Jesus. They put other people's needs before their own. All the good things they did were not to make themselves feel important, but to praise God.

I'm sure everyone here knows someone who is now in Heaven — someone who loved Jesus very much and is now with Jesus in Heaven. Even though we cannot see that person any more, we know we are all connected with the love we have for Jesus.

You see numbers around the room. They are the years that some of our great saints died and went to Heaven. Some of the years are a very long time ago when the world was certainly different, but in all of those years there were great saints. Those saints are praying for us now, and we remember them today.

We are going to read a little about 10 saints, and there is an item on each table that represents one of them. We will have one person bring up that item and put it next to the year on the time line. That shows we are a community of saints!

So that all of us remember the saints, and how special they are, we have stickers to represent each saint, and you can put them into the little booklet of saints on your table.

Do you think that you will work hard to be a saint? Each of us can do that, and then, maybe in a hundred years, someone will be talking about us.

First, **St. John the Baptist** (30): He wore rough clothing and led a simple life. Is there a piece of burlap on your table? He wanted everyone to pray and to get ready for Jesus' coming. (Sticker is praying hands.)

St. Peter (65): He was a fisherman. Is there something a fisherman would use on someone's table? (Fishing pole or net.) He was one of the Apostles, one of Jesus' best friends. The picture of Jesus is the one to remember Peter in your booklet.

St. Nicholas (342): There are stories that St. Nicholas loved children so much, he used to put candy in their shoes! In certain countries in the world, people still do this to remember St. Nicholas. Would someone bring up the Christmas candy? The Christmas sticker goes on his page in your booklet.

St. Patrick (461): St. Patrick is known for the shamrock. He saw that the three leaves on the one plant could symbolize the three persons of God: the Father, Son, and the Holy Spirit. The sticker for St. Patrick is the shamrock.

St. Francis of Assisi (1226): How many of you know about St. Francis? Every year in October, we have a blessing of our pets to remember how much St. Francis loved animals. Are there animals on your table? His sticker is the animal sticker.

St. Juan Diego (1548): St. Juan met Mary, the Mother of Jesus, and she asked him to build a beautiful church where she was standing. As a sign to him that she was really the Mother of Jesus, she put her picture, surrounded by flowers and stars, on the inside of his coat. Is there a black cloth with stars on it? His sticker is a star. Mary's image was surrounded by stars.

St. Martin de Porres (1639): He grew up very poor and had a hard life. It was said that he worked tirelessly healing people, and he opened orphanages to take care of children. He loved all God's people and all creatures. Is there a medical kit? His sticker is the heart.

St. Vincent de Paul (1660): He was a priest who was most known for his generosity to others. "GIVE" was the word that best describes his daily life. He happily worked very hard raising money and taking care of the poor. Is there a bag of coins to represent how much he gave to the poor? His sticker is a smiley face for the happiness he brought to sad people.

Bl. Kateri (1680): She was an American Indian who knew that God was calling her to be a Christian and to be baptized. Life was not easy for her because none of her family followed Jesus. She had a great devotion for the rosary. Is there a rosary? Her sticker is the cross.

St. Thérèse (1873): She was often called the "Little Flower" because hers was the little way, doing little things every day for Jesus. When she died, she promised to drop a shower of roses down from Heaven. Are there roses on your table? Flower stickers go on her page.

Our faith tells us that when we pray to the saints for special things in our lives, they pray to Jesus for us. They connect our prayers to Jesus.

Many miracles throughout the last 2000 years have happened because people asked the saints to pray for them.

On the last page of your booklet, it says, "Yes, WE CAN ALL BE SAINTS TOO!" Put Jesus first in your life, and always pray to Him. You may keep this book to remember the saints.

Next, we have our PARISH POND, so each child can grab a fishing pole and try his luck at being a fisherman, like St. Peter. Let's see what kind of fish are in the Parish Pond!

In the craft area, we have a lot of materials to make a mask. What kind of face do you want to present to the world?

Script Supplies:

Timeline:

- 8.5" x11" sheets of paper, each one printed with one large, bold date of a saint's death (30, 65, 342, 461, 1226, 1548, 1639, 1660, 1680, and 1873) taped to the wall in chronological order
- Symbolic items to distribute among the tables where the families are seated: A piece of burlap, a fishing pole or a net, candy canes, large felt or foam shamrocks, a stuffed animal, a piece of black cloth with stars on it, a doctor's bag or a stethoscope, a bag of coins, a rosary, and silk roses.
- Saint booklet template to copy for each family (See pages 187–191. Cut pages in half on the dotted line; fasten together with paper fasteners, staples, or hole punch and tie with yarn.)
- Stickers: flowers, crosses, smiley faces, hearts, stars, animals, shamrocks, Christmas, Jesus, "praying hands" (complete sets in sufficient numbers so that each child can fill in his or her own booklet)

Fishpond Supplies:

- Blue sheet or large blue paper with pictures of fish pinned to it, hung 3' to 4' over a coat-rack or similar structure
- Bamboo poles or dowels, 18" to 24" long (fishing poles) tied with about the same length of string
- Large paperclips or small magnets ("hooks")
- A helper, hidden behind the pond to slip small prizes onto the hooks.
- "Fish" (Prizes): Stickers, candy, holy cards, coloring pages, etc.

Mask Craft Supplies:

- Materials to make masks: paper plates, Popsicle sticks, glue, tape, scissors, crayons or markers, yarn, buttons, felt scraps, and some examples.
- A sign that says:

  Are you …
  Gentle as a Lamb?
  Courageous as a Lion?
  Curious as a Cat?
  Loyal as a Dog?
  Sly as a Fox?
  Busy as a Beaver?
  Wise as an Owl?
  Fast as a Cheetah?
  Agile as a Monkey?
  Strong as an Ox?
  Happy as a Lark?
  Free as a Bird?

  Make a mask to show a good quality about yourself!

Animal mask example

Refreshments:

If possible, this is a great time to serve a variety of different ethnic snacks to remind the families that saints represent our world community.

Beverages

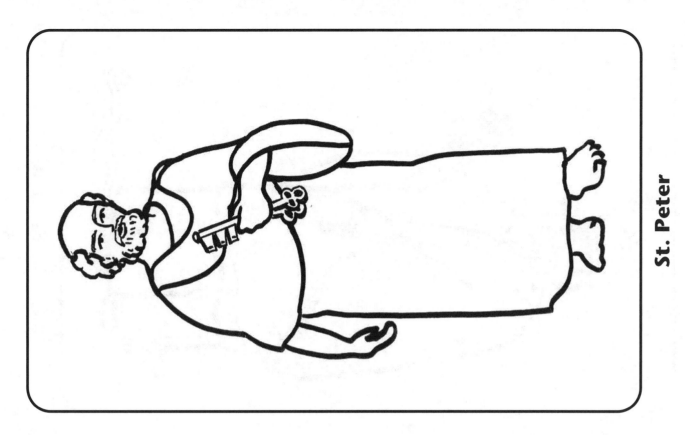

St. Peter

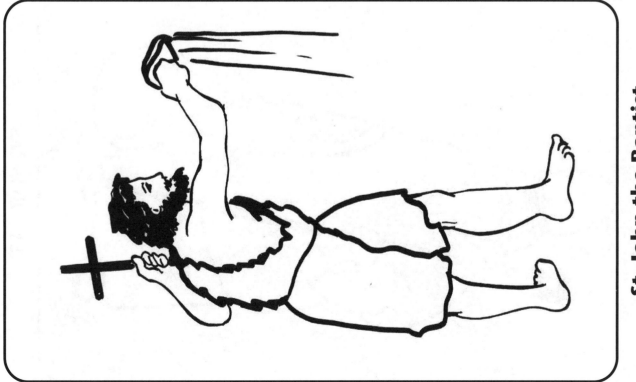

St. John the Baptist

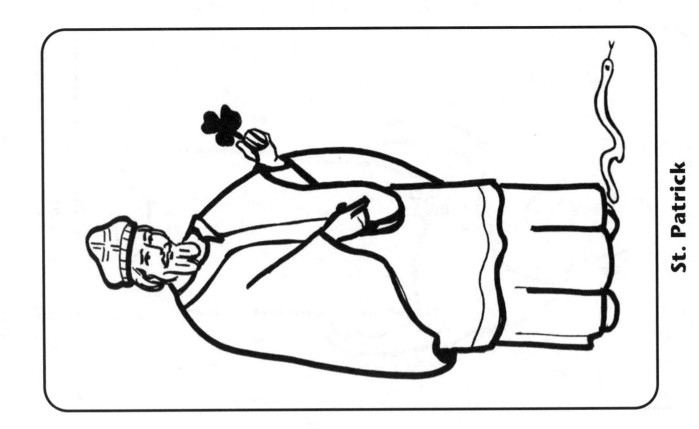

St. Patrick

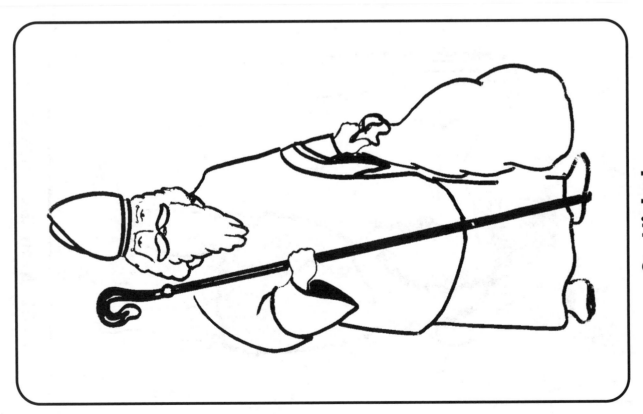

St. Nicholas

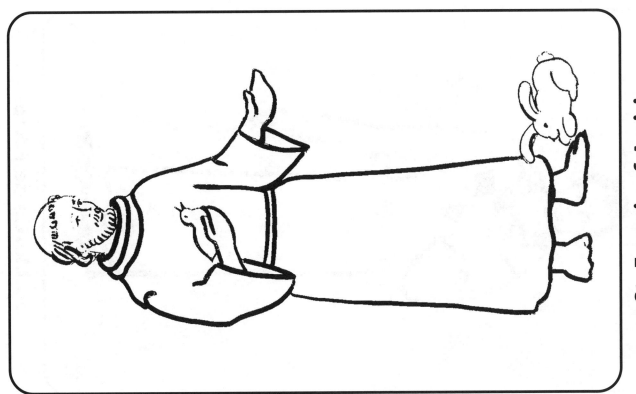

St. Juan Diego

St. Francis of Assisi

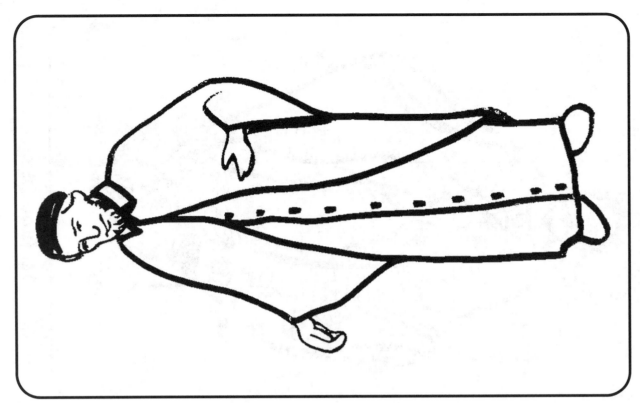

St. Vincent de Paul

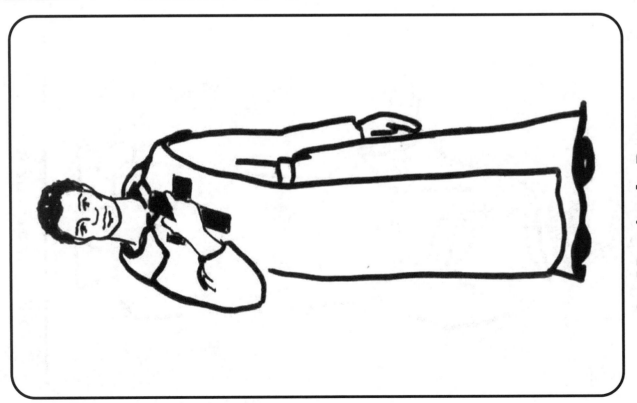

St. Martin de Porres

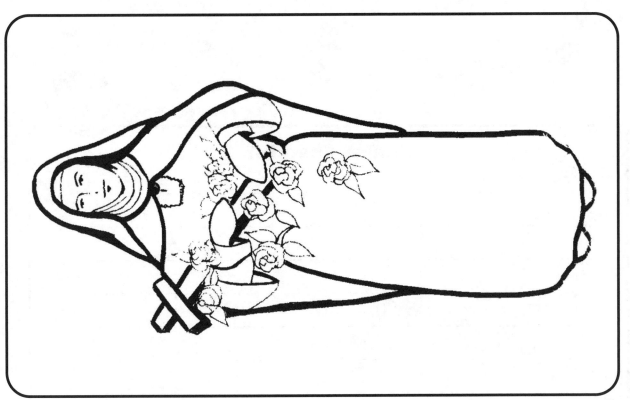

St. Thérèse

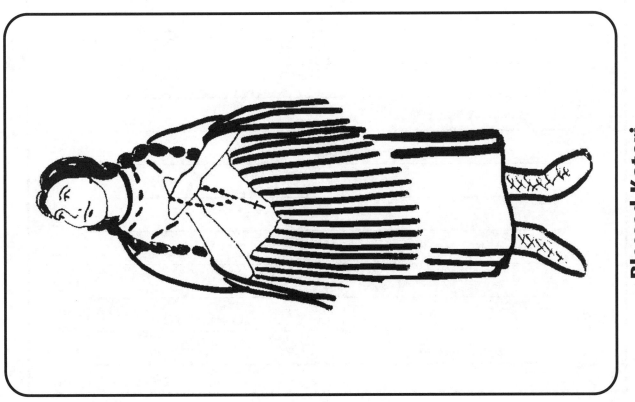

Blessed Kateri

Project Checklist

_____
_____
_____
_____
_____
_____
_____
_____
_____
_____
_____
_____
_____
_____
_____
_____
_____
_____
_____
_____
_____

22. THANKSGIVING

Objective:

To provide families the opportunity for reflection on the many blessings of their lives.

Activity Summary:

The families are invited to remember and write down specific things they are grateful for on the fruit and vegetable picture cutouts (patterns provided or magazine pictures taped on index cards) in the center baskets on their tables. These fruits and vegetables are taped on a large empty cornucopia displayed on a wall. Every family says their own prayer when they put their blessings on the Horn of Plenty. Following this, the crafts are displayed and all are asked to enjoy the projects. The three crafts are an American Indian prayer wheel, a bird feeder, and a "Family Talk" book to take home. At the close of the Gathering, there is a paper wreath on the wall, and a variety of colored construction papers and markers. The parents are asked to trace a handprint of their child's hand, and write down what they love about him/her the most. Then they glue it on the wreath. This wreath could be displayed on a wall in the meeting room for future Gatherings or placed in Church.

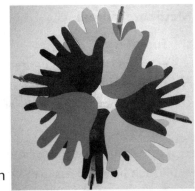

Handprint wreath

Activity Setting:

A paper drawing of a large, empty cornucopia is on a wall in the meeting area. The tables each have a basket with cutout pictures of fruits and vegetables and markers. The craft tables have been covered for protection and have all needed items on them. The refreshment table is set with coffee, cider, and donuts.

Script:

Welcome, everyone, to our Thanksgiving Family Gathering! This is the season when we take a few minutes, like we will do today, and think about how great God is! On your tables are baskets of cutout fruits and vegetables. On the wall you can see a Horn of Plenty — we are going to fill it with all the blessings we want to thank God for. How many of you are most grateful for your loving family? Or your warm home and regular meals? Or friends to play with? Or your computer games? Or doctors and dentists? Or school? Or Church? Or beautiful sunny days with the leaves changing colors outside? Or a pet? We invite you to talk over your blessings, and write them on the fruits and vegetables and then tape them on the Horn of Plenty. When you tape it on, say a short prayer of thankfulness to God!

Thanksgiving

Our crafts today are an American Indian prayer wheel; a bird feeder; and a little book called "Family Talk" that we ask every family to use at dinner each night. Everyone has to answer the same question — even Mom, Dad, Grandmother, and Grandfather!

Remember that the last time we were together, we asked you to bring a "table blessing" or "dinner grace" today? If you did that, please place the prayer in this basket. We are going to take all your blessings and put them in a book that you can take home the next time you come.*

Thank you and enjoy doing your crafts!

You may or may not wish to add this activity to the Gathering. If you do, introduce it at the previous Gathering by inviting families to bring in a copy of their favorite meal grace. At this Gathering, collect the prayers in order to create a "Parish Meal Grace Booklet."

Crafts Supplies and Instructions:

Medicine Wheel

Supplies
- Paper plate with center cut out
- Craft sticks, glue, markers, hole punch
- Yarn, beads, and feathers

Directions
Glue craft sticks across the center opening to form a cross.
Punch four holes along bottom half of wheel.
Thread yarn through hole.
Tie beads or feathers to yarn.
Color one end of a stick red, one blue, one green, one yellow.
Add color or drawing to border of wheel.

Bird Feeder

Supplies
- Rice cakes, peanut butter, seeds, and string

Directions:
Poke a hole into the rice cake and thread the string through to hang.
Spread peanut butter liberally, pat birdseed on.

Family Talk Book:
Using the provided template, copy and cut pages apart, then attach at the corners with paper fasteners.

Refreshments:
Coffee, cider, and donuts

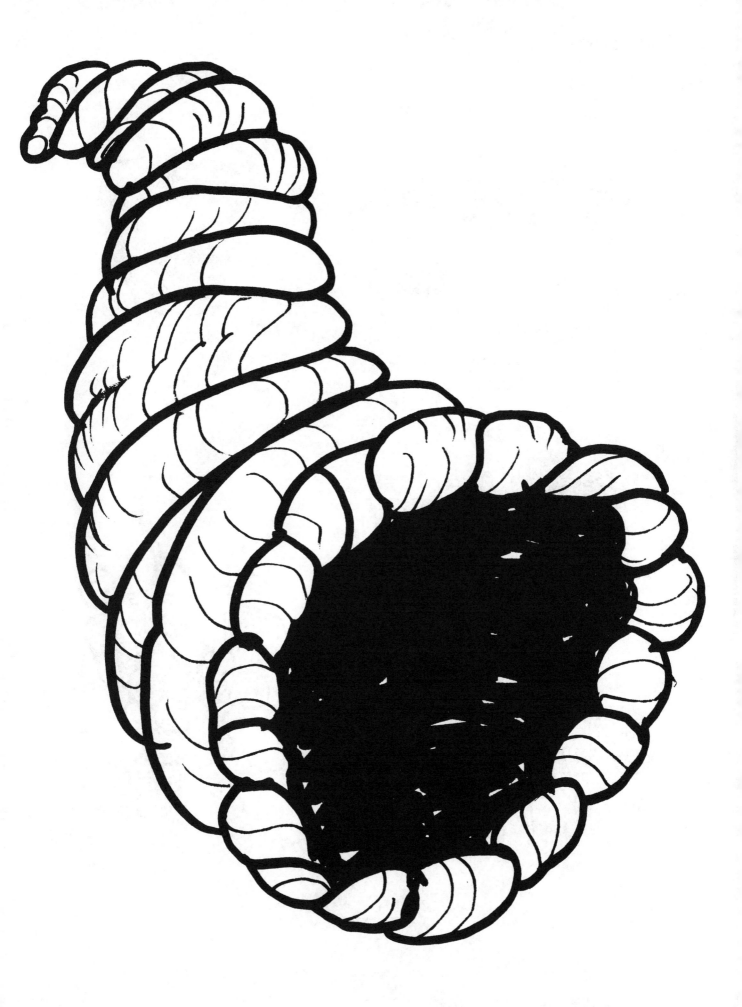

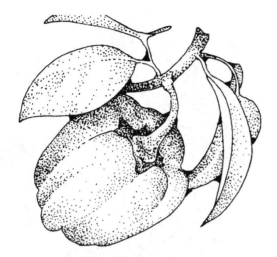

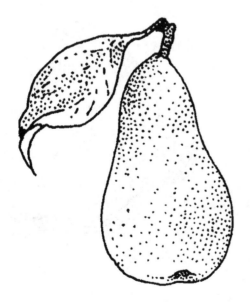

Family Talk . . .

When I don't get
my way I . . .

My favorite school
memory is . . .

If I could marry someone
famous, I would marry . . .

The most important quality
I look for in a friend is . . .

I complain a lot about . . .

In three years, I will be different than I am today in these ways . . .

The most beautiful thing that I have ever seen is . . .

People would like me better if . . .

The world problem I am most concerned with is . . .

A birthday or holiday that I'll always remember is . . .

I wish I could change . . .

Sometimes I
wonder why . . .

It upsets me when . . .

Of all my senses (smelling, seeing,
touching, hearing, or tasting)
I like _____ the best
because . . .

I think the most difficult thing
Jesus told us to do is . . .

The smile I most remember
today is . . .

I hope I never . . .

When I have free time,
I like to . . .

I think Jesus looked like . . .

If I could be someone else in
my family, it would be . . .

A person who's taught me a lot
is _____ because . . .

My favorite movie of
all time is . . .

A time I felt proud . . .

If I could leave anything
in my will to my best friend,
I would leave . . .

Some day I hope to . . .

Three words to describe
me are . . .

If I could go anywhere
I wish on a vacation,
I would go . . .

I admire people who . . .

The best day of my life
so far was . . .

Project Checklist

23. "OTHER PEOPLE'S SHOES"

Theme:
Disability Awareness

Objective:
To understand some physical disabilities and the challenges they pose.

Setting:
A large, open area with a sign: "Disability Sim Center," is prepared with crutches, a wheelchair, blindfolds, slings, etc., for the children to experience being physically disabled. There is also a hallway prepared with a few soft obstacles (cardboard boxes or chairs) marked "Trust Walk." A table has a large sign that says, "Look closely, we are alike, but different" and serves as the center for an ink pad craft.

A table is set up with chopsticks or straws and bowls containing cotton balls or miniature marshmallows, and another table has cookies or candy that are individually wrapped in many layers of paper and several oven mitts.

Lastly, an artist area (easels, tables, or large papers taped to the wall) provides brushes and washable paints or large crayons and paper (taped down so that it doesn't move around) for the children to draw without using their hands or blindfolded. If desired, there is a craft area with construction paper, markers, and a variety of small items (foam cutouts and letters, stickers, etc.) to make greeting cards to send to a Veterans Hospital or rehabilitation facility.

Activity Summary:
A speaker gives a short presentation on how people cope with different physical challenges. (It works best if someone who is physically impaired, their parent, a nurse or doctor can address this as well as show the families how to maneuver a wheel chair or walker, put on a brace, etc.). Then the children with their parents are free to travel between the "Disability Sim Area," the "Trust Walk," and the craft areas. Catechists are available in all areas to assist. The first activity offers ways for the children to try crutches, wheelchairs, walkers, etc., to get a feel for some of the limitations that other people have to face. To appreciate the difficulties of impaired coordination, a table is set with chopsticks for the children to try to pick up cotton balls (or marshmallows). Nearby, another table challenges them to unwrap treats (wrapped in multiple layers of paper) with oven mitts on their hands. An artist area is also set up for the children to try to

paint or draw without using their hands (an alternative is drawing while blindfolded). The craft is an activity where the children "ink their thumbprint" and then compare it with others using a magnifying glass. If desired, there is an additional table supplied with items to create greeting cards for patients in a nearby Veterans Hospital or rehabilitation facility.

Script:

Welcome to our Family Gathering! As you can see by looking around, we have a lot going on here today — what do you recognize over in this area? *(Narrator walks over to the Disability Sim Area.)* In our families, our neighborhoods, in school, church, shopping, wherever we go, we often see people who have different physical abilities than we have. Whereas running down a street, tying gym shoes, throwing a ball, or simply eating dinner comes so easily to most of us, there are many people who struggle or are simply not able to do these things without help. Moving their arms and legs and hands, seeing clearly, hearing what is being said around them, is very difficult! Today, we are going to try to put you in someone else's shoes. We have borrowed wheelchairs, walkers, braces, crutches, etc., for you to try on, and there is someone in that area to help you. There is also a "Trust Walk" hallway — what do you think that means? With a partner, you can practice walking as if you were blind. (We have someone there to help also.)

On another table we have activities to help us realize how difficult it is to do simple things, such as eating, when our hands don't move freely. There is a lot here to keep you busy today. Please, families, stay together through the activity areas, and take time to talk at home about what you experienced. Our craft today helps us see that even though we look very much the same in many ways, there is one thing that easily identifies us — there is no one else that has it "just the same" as ours — our thumbprint! We have an ink pad in the craft area and magnifying glasses. Take a look and see that your thumbprint is different from everyone else's! We have a craft table also for you to make greeting cards for people who struggle with these same things you are going to experience today — people in hospitals who are learning to live differently because of a physical change in their body. If you would like to make a card, we will make sure they receive them!

Activity Supplies:
- Crutches, wheelchair, slings, blindfolds, dowels, and tape or scarves
- A few large, soft "obstacles" for the "Trust Walk"
- Chopsticks and bowls with miniature marshmallows or cotton balls
- Oven mitts, cookies, or candy that is individually wrapped in 5 to 8 layers of paper

Artist Area Crafts Supplies and Instructions:

Supplies
- Ink pads, poster board, small sheets of paper
- Magnifying glasses
- Sign saying, "Look closely, we are alike, but different!"
- Washable paints and brushes or large crayons (one for each child)

- Easels or tables with large paper
- Old shirts to protect clothes if using paint
- Construction paper, markers, stickers, cutout foam shapes and letters

Directions

Ink Pad Area
Children ink their thumbprint on a poster board.
They compare it with others by using a magnifying glass.

Art Area
The children draw or paint either blindfolded or without using their hands (if this is done, individual brushes are needed for the children to use and then take home — as the brushes will most likely be held by their clenched teeth!).

Greeting Card
Children/families create greeting cards from the available supplies to send to an area Veterans Hospital or rehabilitation facility.

Refreshments:
Small individual cups of snack mixes (Chex or Gorp)
Multicolored napkins and cups

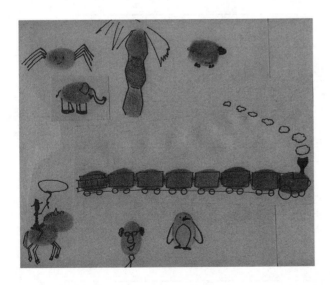 

Thumbprint examples: After the children compare their thumbprints to see how similar we are but still unique, provide paper and crayons to embellish additional thumbprints into scenes, animals, and people.

Project Checklist

Topical Index

Index

Index

W

Notes

Notes